The Holy Way

Cathryn Lucille Easley

TRAFFORD
PUBLISHING

Order this book online at www.trafford.com
or email orders@trafford.com

Most Trafford titles are also available at major online book retailers.

Picture Credits:
141 The exaltation of the Holy Cross, drawn by Omar Easley.
142 The sorrowful heart of Mary. Drawn by Quentin Easley

Printed in the United States of America.

ISBN: 978-1-4269-6285-1 (sc)
ISBN: 978-1-4269-6286-8 (e)

Library of Congress Control Number: 2011905572

Trafford rev. 05/16/2011

 www.trafford.com

North America & international
toll-free: 1 888 232 4444 (USA & Canada)
phone: 250 383 6864 ♦ fax: 812 355 4082

A NEW SIGN
The Messianic Seal
Of the Church Of Jerusalem

"Recently, a remarkable discovery has taken place in Israel. A symbol was discovered on pottery used by the early Church. Among the artifacts recently discovered bearing this symbol is a brick-shaped piece of local marble inscribed with the Messianic seal and the words in Aramaic; "For the Oil of the Spirit."

This piece of marble seems to have been the base for a vial of anointing oil. A small pottery piece with the same Messianic seal was found nearby. These were found, along with some sixty others, in a grotto now called the Sacred Baptismal Grotto of James the Just and the Apostles on Mount Zion in Jerusalem. James the brother of Jesus was the leader of the first-century believers in Jerusalem. Their place of worship was believed to be on Mount Zion.

In 1990, Ludwig Schneider, editor-in-chief of the magazine Israel Today struck up a friendship with an old Greek Orthodox monk who lives as a hermit in the Old City of Jerusalem. One day the monk showed Schneider a cache of artifacts that he had secretly excavated on Mount Zion before the Six-Day War in 1967. Schneider was taken aback. Many of these pottery shards, oil lamps and stone pieces were engraved with an unknown symbol. The symbol consisted of a menorah at the top, a Star of David in the center, and a fish at the bottom.

Schneider was immediately convinced that this must have been a symbol of the first Jewish-Christian congregation.

The monk then led Schneider to a cavity in the rock adjacent to the Tomb of David and the Upper Room on Mount Zion and told him that this is where he found the artifacts. Today, the cave is dark and musty and sealed off with iron bars. These would have been the earliest known artifacts from the Church.

Today, we often use the fish symbol on bumper stickers on our cars. Many do this without even wondering where it originated. The fish symbol, however, is only half of the truth. The other half was cut out of Christian symbols, along with everything else Jewish, after the Council of Nicaea in A.D. 325. The menorah and the Star of David belong with the fish to form the entire symbol.

The fish, in that sense, has become a symbol of our lack. We are running on only half the power, revelation and unity that the early Church knew. As we plug the pieces back together (much like a key is inserted to turn the ignition and start an engine), the power God intended us to have will come roaring back. As we allow God to combine the Jewish and Gentile believers into one Body, we will begin to walk in the fullness of what has been reserved for us." (Mysteries of the Glory Unveiled. By David Herzog). To me this New Sign represents Jews and Christians coming together, to make up the New Jerusalem, I believe this is what God is calling all of His children to understand, so that we all may be at peace and one in the Body of Christ, to the Glory of our Father, Amen.

Cover Credits

Article courtesy of *Israel Today* magazine by Ludwig Schneider, Editor-in-Chief

Book cover from a book called *Mysteries of the Glory Unveiled* by David Herzog

TABLE OF CONTENTS

ACKNOWLEDGMENT

With all my love I want to thank Father Larry Baumann for all his kindness in helping me. Also, Barry at Postnet in Prescott Valley, Arizona. Barry's graphic designer John Nelson. These men have given me their time every time I asked it of them; I would like them to know how much I appreciate all that they have done for me. I have struggled with my grammar, English and my computer skills. Thanks to all their help I was finally able to produce and publish The Holy Way. To you sweet Ronda Tweedy at Mountain Ink, thank you also for your time and help. I love you all and I thank God for you. I also want to tell my mom thank you for all her help and direction.

Thank You, Sincerely

Cathryn Lucille Easley

INTRODUCTION

I finished my Introduction on August 15, 2010. On the Feast day of the Assumption of the Blessed Virgin Mary: Because of the oneness that I share in Christ Jesus through the Holy Spirit, I also share this same love of God for Mary His daughter. This love is unconditional, and always to be cherished. Thank you ever Virgin Mary for being such a wonderful example to God's children that we might learn to walk with God sinless, and joyfully learn to follow in your footsteps. "May we be drawn after you in the fragrance of your holiness?" (Little Office of the Blessed Virgin Mary: Page 34). "Father, source of light in every age, the Virgin conceived and bore your Son who is called Wonderful God, Prince of Peace. May her prayer, the gift of a mother's love, be your people's joy through all ages? May her response, born of a humble heart, draw your Spirit to rest on your people? Grant this through Christ our Lord. May the Lord bless us, protect us from all evil and bring us to everlasting life. Amen." (Little Office of the Blessed Virgin Mary: Page 23). I love you Queen of Heaven as a Daughter, Sister and my Mother. I have found you being faithful and true always there interceding for the living and the dead. My life with you and the Trinity, in heaven on earth is true life; I have been given the way, the truth and life with and in Jesus Christ Crucified in the Unity of the Holy Spirit and in God's Almighty Power. I truly look forward to eternity in heaven with you and all God's family. I sincerely thank you, for our many blessings and for the life we find in your Son Jesus Christ. So in this way we are offering all to God through the hands of the Blessed Virgin Mary. +

"In faith and love we ask you, Father, to watch over your family gathered here. In your mercy and loving kindness no thought of ours is left unguarded, no tear unheeded, no joy unnoticed. Through the prayer of Jesus may the blessings promised to the poor in spirit lead us to the treasures of your heavenly kingdom. We ask this in the name of Jesus the Lord." (Divine Office page 249). +

As the Father, Son and Holy Spirit are helping us pull the plank out of our eyes so we can see and understand God's kingdom on earth. That by pulling the plank out of our eyes we might turn from our evil ways and live as God does. As we are pulling the plank out of our eyes Our Lord is telling us that we need to remove it so we might see and understand what He has done for us. Nothing defiled can enter Our Lord' Kingdom. +

In the Resurrection of Jesus Christ Crucified and the coming of our Savior we the living and the dead that are experiencing spiritual and or physical death are being restored to our principle of life and given sanctifying grace through the exercise of Jesus Christ Crucified, in God's Almighty Power. +

"Everyone who sins, dies," says St. Augustine. "Only the Lord, "by His great grace and great mercy raises souls to life again, that we may not die eternally" Only infinite mercy can reconcile the grave sinner." (Modern Catholic Dictionary, John A. Hardon, S. J. Page 515). As we are being raised or resurrected by Jesus Christ Crucified in God's Almighty Power from our spiritual and or our physical death, our bodies are still on earth and this union with God is both a possession and a movement, we possess Jesus by grace and by faith and we are moving toward Him in the Beatific Vision of glory. And we the living and the dead can ascend to the Throne in our Lord and Savior's glorious body spiritually and physically. And this is how we the living and the dead can live and experience death in the new heaven and new earth with everlasting life. +

"But even as it is written, they who have not been told of Him shall see, and they who have not heard shall understand." (Romans 15:21). In our human existence we are not experiencing eternal death only spiritual and physical death. And in this way we can be given everlasting life in the New Heaven and New Earth. +

For the love of God and the love of my children and their children's children, and all God's children I have written this book. I have written to you the hearer, of the things pertaining to Our Father, His Son the Holy Spirit and of our Heavenly Mother. And also about the gifts to us, which is the way, the truth and life. They are all spiritual gifts, things people cannot steal nor destroy. And when you find them, they will bring you much peace, joy and happiness in the new heaven and new earth. When we embrace the Holy Way we are also embracing Holy Love and Holy Love leads us into the New Jerusalem. +

"God's saving action as summed up in the Isaiah story continues to be repeated throughout our lives. We are constantly being delivered from death to life if we are willing to cooperate. Change, especially when it is thrust upon us rather than chosen, is rarely welcomed. We can feel anxious and even angry and resist the very things that will eventually prove to be life-giving. Worst of all, we so desperately want to hold on to the way things used to be that we entirely miss the gifts to be found in the present moment." (Spurgeon's devotional). +

Heavenly Father, give us eyes to see the wonder of your faithfulness and your truthfulness. I hope and pray that this message will reach the Pope and all God's children wherever they may be, that we can receive it as food and share it with all God's children, enabling them to have bright futures. +

And yes this can be a struggle, but it can be done. So with all respect and honor we come with thankful hearts to our Maker. Rejoicing: in all our blessings and our spiritual gifts of everlasting life with and in Jesus Christ Crucified. And we do this in the Unity of the Holy Spirit all through God's Almighty Power. All glory and honor to Our God, the Father Almighty in heaven and earth, Amen. The rain is cleansing the world, the sun is shining and all things are growing with and in you Lord, through the Holy Spirit. Thank you: Father, Son and Holy Spirit for all life with and in you. +

Chapter 1

Dear Papa your Holiness

I want to say Thank You for all your Love and Devotion and hopefully your time. What I have to say is very spiritual and hard to believe, but true.

In l985 a priest Father Al Dawe from St. Peter's Episcopal Church, Casa Grande, Arizona did some work on me giving the anointing of the sick, and cleansing me. Then he said that we are going to meditate. During the mediation it was as if I was no longer with the priest. I was on a river bank with Jesus and he walked out of the clouds to me. Our Lord was wearing a long white rode with a royal blue covering. And the first thing he said to me was "For God so loved the world that he gave his only begotten Son, that whosoever believeth in him should not perish, but have everlasting life." (John 3:16.) Then he told me about my future and it was shocking. +

I could hear very beautiful music. Then two girls appeared wearing long white robes, walking in the clouds with a boy between them and he was colorful all over, I could see through him. Jesus said that the boy had fallen asleep, or that he had died and that he had to take him to his Father in Heaven. +

So when Jesus walked away I was present with the priest again. The priest asked me whether I had seen Jesus. All that I could remember was that Jesus told me that He loved me.

A couple of years later I met Billy my boyfriend. We were together for a couple of years before the veil was lifted, then I remembered everything pertaining to my vision. The person (J   Christ) in my vision looked just like Billy. +

Papa I was very scared and didn't know what to do. I was living a very corrupt life and continued in that life for fifteen years. During those fifteen years I started reading the Bible. While praying and fasting one day God the Father drew me to Him in a dream, but I was awake.

In this dream I saw God the Father; I learned later that he looked like Saint Vincent De Paul only with more hair. He was saying: "who wants to go to earth and be Billy's girlfriend" "And I said: "I do." +

So God the Father drew me to Himself. All that I could see was God the Father. He started telling of my future as if I hadn't been born yet. Then I saw the earth with Billy's face and Jesus Christ face they were the same in front of the earth. Their faces were the same face that I saw in my vision when I saw Christ. So when I came back to my senses I felt a lot better about being with Billy. No longer "woe is me," but praising God. +

The man (God the Father) I met in my dream also looked just like a person I met in Farmington, New Mexico. His name is Ron Miller. I believe God the Father was manifested in him. Using the word manifested is the only way I know how to describe the presence of God. I was at his place one day in a travel trailer very scared. And I looked out the window and I could see him. A bush was on fire. Then Ron Miller (God the Father manifested) left and I went outside and looked and the bush was there, but no fire. It had not been consumed. +

God the Father who was manifested in Ron Miller also breathed into my mouth several times, as if to give me the Spirit and or life.

My husband and I have 7 children and we are very much in love and are very happy. In the year 2002 I was pregnant sitting in jail with my 7th child. I had the Bible and the Book of Mormon and while I was reading it, I was deprogrammed and reprogrammed. The Lord saved me, through the Word of God, and Jesus Christ Crucified with God's Almighty Power. My mind body soul and spirit was restored. +

The scriptures pertaining to the end of times and Jesus coming are being fulfilled in me spiritually and physically. I died to sin and experienced Spiritual Death at the foot of the cross with Jesus and Mary through the Holy Spirit in God's Almighty Power. At this Spiritual Death I experienced a Divine Intervention and it removed all sin supernaturally. I was washed clean by Jesus' precious blood and I was also baptized by the spirit of fire that is spoken of in the scriptures. And once this occurred I was given the new heaven and new earth. I was redeemed by Jesus Christ in God's Almighty Power. Jesus Christ's body and blood that was poured out for all mankind has bought my salvation. Jesus Christ has restored me to the state of life that Adam and Eve were in before they had sinned. And so in this way I conceived the Holy Spirit and the Word of God without sin. My conception was immaculate, and because of the way I gave birth spiritually to Jesus in me, I remain a virgin spiritually. Thus I received an immaculate heart also. Praise God. +

Not only did Jesus Christ remove all sin, also I have been justified with deeds done in Jesus Christ. He also gave me the light of faith that led me to Divine Mercy. So through the gift of Divine Mercy Jesus gave me His Charity and He forgave me of all the sins I had committed against God and man. Then Fire from heaven came down upon me and I experienced the baptism of Fire, and I was purged of all my sins. God destroyed by fire the root of evil that was in me the world, which causes sin and death to reign. I was no longer spiritually dead, but was resurrected from the grave with Jesus Christ Crucified to a new spiritual life, with and in Jesus Christ's glorified body, the two became one. (There will be two people in a field one will be taken and one will be left, I believed and God was Truthful to His Word, God was Faithful to me and I was taken.) +

The great deceiver was revealed no longer able to deceive me about life and death. The devil was chained up for a thousand years and when I realized that I could never eternally die, death was thrown into the lake of Fire, which produced Life Everlasting in me. Then the New Heaven and New Earth came down from Heaven and I became the Bride of Christ. A New Creation with and in Christ in the here and now. God renewed the face of the earth, on my account, with my free will and my cooperation.

Jesus Christ filled me the living with His Grace. No longer am I lawless. I myself as a Catholic know that I am still a sinner in the sense that I can commit venial sin but the Spiritual Death that I incurred was by Divine Intervention and that Divine Intervention supernaturally restored me to a state of life that can not die, I was given everlasting life in Jesus Christ. And yet I know when I fall asleep in the Lord, I am still living. Sleep is not death for me yet it is the end of my life as I know it, in the here and now. I can only speak of the things I see and the things I hear. I followed Jesus Christ and God gave me the land of my inheritance. And when I come to the end of this life and I fall asleep in the Lord, I know I will be sleeping in the Lord, and that we are united whether I am sleeping or awake. Physical death cannot separate the members of His body. And in this way I can dwell in heaven on earth forever, because when God wakes me from my sleep, and I am resurrected from the dead I believe God gives me life in His kingdom with and in Jesus Christ and all those dwelling with the Father, and because I accepted our Lords gift of life with and in Him, he tells me that he has a place prepared for me. I will be in heaven on earth because we are still united as one living and loving and never dieing, thus interceding for the living and the dead in heaven on earth. +

Because I experienced spiritual death with Jesus Christ the New Heaven and New Earth came down from Heaven. I became the Bride of Christ. I rejoice in Jerusalem, for through you all men will be gathered to the Lord. In my Fathers goodness He has shown favor to Zion; He is rebuilding the walls of Jerusalem. Jerusalem, city of God, where I dwell you shine with a radiant light, alleluia. (There is no more wailing wall for me). Only rejoicing. My maiden name is Wall. "He showed me the holy city Jerusalem which shone with the glory of God". (Revelation 21:10-11). +

"Let all men speak of the Lord's majesty, and sing his praises in Jerusalem. O Jerusalem, holy city, he scourged you for the works of your hands, but will again pity the children of the righteous.

Praise the Lord for his goodness, and bless the King of the ages, so that his tent may be rebuilt in you with joy.

May he gladden within you all who were captives; all who were ravaged may he cherish within you for all generations to come.

A bright light will shine to all parts of the earth; many nations shall come to you from afar, and the inhabitants of all the limits of the earth, drawn to you by the name of the Lord God, bearing in their hands their gifts for the King of heaven.

Every generation shall give joyful praise in you, and shall call you the chosen one, through all ages forever.

Go, then, rejoice over the children of the righteous, who shall be gathered together and shall bless the Lord of the ages.

Happy are those who love you, and happy those who rejoice in your prosperity.

Happy are all the men who shall grieve over you, over all your chastisements, for they shall rejoice in you as they behold all your joy forever. My spirit blesses the Lord, the great King." (Tobit 13:8-11, 13-15.) +

The Zion within me praises my God, who sent His Word to renew the face of the earth. So by the baptism of fire my world ended spiritually and physically with and in Jesus Christ Crucified and through the Holy Spirit and by the exercise of God's Almighty Power and my co-operation. I was lead by the Word of God to the New Heaven and New Earth and I became the Bride of Christ in the New Jerusalem. +

My two oldest sons look like saints. My son James looks just like James the greater and Jason the Apostle John they are called the Sons of Thunder. I also want you to know that my nineteen year old daughter looks just like our Mother Mary. My son Omar Francis looks just like Francis of Assisi, and another son Quentin looks just like Thomas Aquinas, and my daughter Daisy Rose looks just like Joan of Arc. My youngest daughter Billie Jo II looks just like St. Bridget of Sweden. My brother Gene looks just like the Apostle James the Less. My brother Gene asked me to tell you that he will be taken in the Rapture and that he does not want to suffer. My mom Ann looks just like St. Ann, Mary's mom. And my husband Billy looks just like Christ in my vision. +

I have included pictures in my book for you to enjoy. I also thought it would be interesting if you could see what I see. Because of my state of life with Christ I have been seeing a lot of the invisible and spiritual world. Mark, Peter, Paul, Jude, Matthew, Phillip, Thomas, Simon, John, Luke, Joseph, Mary and lots more, including our Saint Nicholas. The people I am recognizing are said to be dwelling in heaven. +

Our being is made up of matter and spirit and spirit cannot be destroyed. Matter can be changed, but not destroyed. And since our Father is pleased to give me the privilege of the Beatific Vision along with the Beatific Vision of Christ I also am able to see all those living in heaven, although I don't recognize everyone yet, I hope to. I am very grateful for everything God has given me. +

When the first world that is inside of us is destroyed by fire and the New Heaven and New Earth come down, God's kingdom will remain within us and we are enabled to move freely. We have been given Freedom and Liberty. Our Lords Kingdom is not of the world of sin and death, but of life. And we find life in the New Heaven and New Earth. We all can become the Bride of Christ and Jesus likes to share every thing with us. So this also includes things of heaven. It is so beautiful. I know I am experiencing the Beatific Vision in the here and now. +

I would like to quote from the Catechism of the Catholic Church. These words are also part of the profession of my faith. "O my God, Trinity whom I adore, help me forget myself entirely so to establish myself in you, unmovable and peaceful as if my soul were already in eternity. May nothing be able to trouble my peace or make me leave you, O my unchanging God, but may each minute bring me more deeply into your mystery! Grant my soul peace. Make it your heaven, your beloved dwelling and the place of your rest. May I never abandon you there, but may I be there, whole and entire, completely vigilant in my faith, entirely adoring, and wholly given over to your creative action." (ccc. # 2565) I am proclaiming nothing less than this. All my prayers were answered. +

I have included a picture of Jesus Christ and what He looked like in my vision. Except that Jesus wasn't wearing the Crown of Thorns in my vision. I attached a picture of Billy my husband to show what I had seen. I find myself being drawn from earthly matters to heavenly glory. There is also one picture in <u>www.allposters.com</u> the number is 6805975 that contains pictures of Hurby, Moses and Aaron together, and the picture of Aaron looks just like our Father in Heaven. And the picture of Moses looks like Jesus, and Hurby reminds me of Hurb Ron Millers brother in Farmington, New Mexico. I hope you enjoy them as much as I do. In this book I have also included pictures of people I know and love, that look like Saints and Prophets, Prophetesses and Martyrs and the Blessed. Not only do I think they look like them I believe it is them. In these last days God has raised up these chosen people to welcome us into His Kingdom, which is Heaven on Earth World without end, Amen. If you go to <u>www.allposters.com</u> you can type in the saint' name and see they still look the same.

I was told by people at Church that we cannot go to heaven until we physically die. But I also believe that we the living and the dead at the coming of Jesus Christ are the people that can be given a new spiritual life with and in Jesus Christ Crucified with God's Almighty Power. And that the dead will be woken from sleep in the Resurrection of Jesus Christ, with God's Almighty Power and can be given life in heaven. I believe that we the living when Jesus comes can apply our Free Will and choose not to wait for physical death to experience the new heaven and new earth. We the living can die to sin and experience spiritual death with Jesus Christ. The two have become one in death. Oneness in the unity of the Holy Spirit is resurrected with Jesus Christ Crucified and we can be given a new spiritual life with and in Jesus Christ Crucified through God's Almighty Power. We can unite as one in mind, body, soul and spirit and we can be healed, by our Savior Jesus Christ, Amen. We the living and the dead are the members of His body, Jesus Christ is the Head. We the living and the dead can ascend to the Throne in Jesus Christ' glorified body spiritually and physically. We the living and the dead can experience eternal life through Jesus Christ Crucified, with God's Almighty Power. We the living and the dead can be given the things of heaven in the here and now, and forever more. God our Father is Spirit and Truth. So I find myself in a heavenly place with people that are vivacious in the presence of God. 1. Full of life and animation; spirited; lively. Long-lived; hard to kill or destroy. And I also know that Jesus Christ is waiting for the living to say to Him "yes," Come Lord Jesus." The living can seek God and His kingdom. Then all things will be given unto them. Jesus and Mary are waiting on us to open our hearts to them, so Jesus can heal our mind, body, soul and spirit. +

Because of the enormous wealth that I received from Jesus through the Holy Spirit from God, I am bound by love to share all things with my brothers and sisters that they might also obtain the wealth being offered. I found it to be very good. That unbelievers and sinners: might reap from this work and experience God's promises, and His spiritual gifts in their hearts and their lives, in the here and now and forever more. +

My husband suggested to me to write to you and tell you about my vision and dream; I am much honored to bring to you the Good News and to share my Joy with you. I love being Catholic; (my mom's family has always been Catholic). I pray that the Father will give you light from Heaven to discern my vision and dream. When I was about 7 years old I had a man all colorful appear in my room and He said Do Not Be Afraid, but I screamed and He disappeared. +

My only desire is that we can bring the flock to the fullness of Truth, and Oneness in Christ Jesus. With much appreciation: and a hope for a response soon. +

Chapter 2

SECRET SINS –"Thou hast set our iniquities before thee, our secret sins in the light of thy countenance." (Ps.90.8 KJV).

"Now you, mortal, say to the house of Israel, Thus you have said: "Our transgressions and our sins weigh upon us, and we waste away because of them; how then can we live?"

Say to them, As I live, says the Lord God, I have no pleasure in the death of the wicked, but that the wicked turn from their ways and live; turn back, turn back from your evil ways; for why will you die, O house of Israel?

And you, mortal, say to your people, The righteousness of the righteous shall not save them when they transgress, and as for the wickedness of the wicked, it shall not make them stumble when they turn from their wickedness, and the righteous shall not be able to live by their righteousness when they sin.

Though I say to the righteous that they shall surely live, yet if they trust in their righteousness and commit iniquity, none of their righteous deeds shall be remembered; but in the iniquity that they have committed they shall die.

Again, though I say to the wicked, "You shall surely die," yet if they turn from their sin and so do what is lawful and right – if the wicked restore the pledge, give back what they have taken by robbery, and walk in the statutes of life, committing no iniquity – they shall surely live, they shall not die.

None of the sins that they have committed shall be remembered against them; they have done what is lawful and right, they shall surely live.

Yet your people say, "The way of the Lord is not just," when it is their own way that is not just. When the righteous turn from their righteousness, and commit iniquity, they shall die for it.

And when the wicked turn from their wickedness, and do what is lawful and right, they shall live by it. Yet you say, "The way of the Lord is not just." O house of Israel, I will judge all of you according to your ways!" (Ezekiel 33:10-20 HBWA – DB, NRSV).

Dear heavenly Father, may we do what you say, and do what you do, in Jesus Christ name, Amen.

I am asking our Father through Jesus Christ Crucified and with Holy Mary, in all the merits of the Saints that have done your will in the unity of the Holy Spirit throughout time to exercise you the world, through the exercise of our Father's Almighty Power and Jesus Christ Crucified. That we the living and the dead may experience death and grief for our sins by the sword (which is the word of God) and experience a spiritual purification with and in Jesus Christ Crucified in God's Almighty Power through the Holy Spirit. That we the world be delivered from evil, and live as the Lord lives.

May all unbeliever's and sinners be drawn by Jesus to the truth. That through this exercise the living and the dead might receive purification of our mind, body, soul and spirit that we would come to the Lord, with sorrow of heart, and truly repent of all our sinful deeds. That the enormous pain we hold in our heart because of sin in our lives, would provoke us to ask God for help to please save us, so in doing so we find ourselves in true repentance, at the foot of the cross in Jerusalem at this moment we actually die to sin with and in our Savior Jesus Christ and we experience spiritual death, with our Lord' death through the Holy Spirit with and in Jesus Christ Crucified through the exercise of God's Almighty Power. That we the hearers be purified and that we may unite in the Holy Spirit in oneness, in our Lord's death and resurrection thus ascend to the Throne with and in our Savior Jesus Christ, thus we the living and the dead will be given everlasting life in the new heaven and new earth. "We are the Lord's poor servants; to Him alone, the living God, we have offered all in sacrifice; we have nothing else to give; we offer him ourselves." (Divine Office Page: 1341) "this is the Canticle in the Divine Office of Zechariah referring to Saint Lucy. Prayer: Lord, give us courage through the prayers of Saint Lucy. Grant this through our Lord Jesus Christ, your Son, who lives and reigns with you and the Holy Spirit, one God, for ever and ever." That we may be found whole in Jesus Christ's body, to the Glory of God at the consummation at the end of time, so that Jesus Christ can present us to His Father from the beginning to the end in great glory. All that is false within us individually will be destroyed by the baptism of fire from the Spirit of Truth. This acceptable offering is for the spiritual purification of our mind, body, soul and spirit only our love of the Trinity and the things of heaven urges us on. We know that faith depends on hearing of the Word, so I the bride of Jesus Christ have come to edify which means to instruct morally and spiritually. I am a true witness of the justice and mercy of God spoken of in the gospels.

JESUS TOLD SIMON PETER "You are Peter and on this rock I will build my church, and the gates of the underworld can never hold out against it. I will give you the keys of the kingdom of heaven…" (Matthew 16:18-19). Words alone do not make you a Christian; you must have words and work's, saying "I accept Jesus Christ as my personal Lord and Savior" does not mean you are saved. In the Bible it is written, "… a person is declared righteous because of actions and not because of faith alone." (James 2:24). The Bible also says that we will be judged by what we have done (Rev. 20:11-15). We need to remember to follow the words which Jesus gave us. "What you do for the least of His people you do for Him…" (Matt. 25:31-46). We are to be baptized and be made disciples. Christ commands us to… make disciples of all nations, baptizing them in the name of the Father, and of the Son, and the Holy Spirit." (Matt. 28:19). "Baptism is spiritual birth, a change from spiritual death to spiritual life, represented as a washing: on both counts it is appropriate for someone conscious of fatal sin to approach baptism." (St. Thomas Aquinas Summa Theologiae Page 585). We need to work the word of God. So that the word of God can be manifested with and in us, through Jesus Christ Crucified and the exercise of God' Almighty Power. So that Jesus and Mary can usher in the New Jerusalem with and in each of us today, and forever more.

I believe the first work or the offering that needs to be done is the Sacrament of the Anointing of the Sick. God's children need this anointing and power from God. All of us are truly sick people; and we need Jesus Christ Crucified and God's Almighty Power in our lives to restore us to our natural state as it was in the beginning. Some of us are living in the Lord, but haven't ascended to the Throne in great glory with and in Jesus Christ Crucified. And some of us are living spiritually dead and don't even know it. The error is due to our unfaithful thinking. We are spiritually dead, only the anointing of the sick and the exercise that is applied through the exercise of God's Almighty Power with and in Jesus Christ Crucified in the unity of Holy Spirit, may we be healed. God can save us but He needs our co-operation, and our free will for the total good of all. With God's help we can be lead to the total good.

"The person who unites his own spiritual death to that of Jesus' death views it as a step towards God and an entrance into everlasting life.

When the Church for the last time speaks Christ's words of pardon and absolution over the dying person, seals him for the last time with a strengthening anointing, and gives him Christ in Viaticum as nourishment for the journey, she speaks gentle assurance: "Go forth," Christian soul from this world in the name of God the Almighty Father, Who created you, in the name of Jesus Christ the Son of the living God, Who suffered for you in the name of the Holy Spirit, who was poured out upon you. Go forth, faithful Christian!

May you live in peace this day, may your home be with God in Zion, with Mary, the virgin Mother of God, with Joseph, and all the angels and saints… May you return to your Creator who formed you from the dust of the earth. May Holy Mary, the angels, and all the saints come to meet you as you go forth from this life? May you see your Redeemer face to face?" (CCC # 1020).

The second work or offering is to unite all the prayers that have been said and will be said from the Rosary and draw from it all it's fruit so that it will produce in us the Passion of Christ and Mary at His Crucifixion.

And from our hearts we will thank everyone for their prayers. Because without them we the world would not be able to obtain the passion that we need to go forth.

And we also want to thank God for the intercession of our Mother Mary's apparitions to all the people she appeared to and told them to pray for unbelievers and for conversion of sinners, and they did what she said, by fasting and praying for us. We have so much to be thankful for. Our hearts should be growing now with appreciation.

The Trinity can heal our mind body soul and spirit. Cure the sickness of our being so that we may grow in holiness through your care. We ask you to restore us to our natural state as it was in the beginning: through Jesus Christ Crucified, and to exercise us with your Almighty Power through the Holy Spirit. No more sin and death, but everlasting life in the new heaven and new earth. We the living can be given everlasting life, and when we fall asleep in death we know we are still living in the Lord, physical death cannot separate the unity we share in Jesus Christ's living body.

We can continue in eternity. Our Father has given us time and it is very precious, we have been given freewill to exercise our path in this life, whether at birth, later in life, or at our passing we have free will. And free will is the gift from God to accept Jesus Christ and all He offers or to reject Him. This is what determines our path in this life, and the life to come in eternity.

When the wind blows it pushes in the direction it blows. If we use our free will as a rudder we can change the way we think and act pertaining to our life.

We don't have to be pushed which ever way the wind is blowing. We can direct our free will in the direction we want to move.

The will of God is the same yesterday, today and tomorrow. Through our free will we can accept Jesus Christ's gift of grace which is saying yes I do believe, you came from heaven, and you're the Son of the Living God and the Son of Mary. "Yes, come Lord Jesus."

Jesus Christ comes to free us from sin and death and to open the gates of heaven to those that would trust in Him, and believe in Him, and follow Him home.

By faith we are to follow the words in Scripture, and by virtue of Jesus Christ Crucified to believe it has been manifested in us through the Holy Spirit in God's Almighty Power. So that God's decrees and promises and our goals are achieved in each generation. And in each generation we can be regenerated.

I believe not all of us at the same time will enter the kingdom of God. Some of us will not taste physical death before the kingdom comes. Enoch walked with God without dieing. Your salvation is a revelation between God and you, no one else is seeing what God is revealing to you at the Coming of Jesus Christ nor do they know the time. When we welcome Jesus into our hearts, the work of the Holy Spirit is personal, and holy, and no one else can see what is taking place in our heart, only God knows the time and day that we will be delivered from our evil ways. What joy we have in our hearts when this occurs: That we might live unto the Lord, in His kingdom in paradise, world without end. Amen, Amen. All praise and glory be to God on High. When we hear of the rapture: we will know that these people have and will be taken, because God has delivered them from evil: That they have been taken to heaven, to live with and in God in heaven, on earth. That they have gone home. And those left here on earth will have a better understanding as to what has taken place: That they may be taken also, in Jesus Name, Amen. May we all learn to cherish the heart and learn what God created it for, in Jesus name, Amen. What rejoicing we have in our hearts at this great Epiphany. The faithful that follow the word know God's will, and are able to understand what He is saying. Just as in Adam all die, so too in Christ shall all be brought to life, but each one in proper order: Christ the first fruits; then, at his coming, those who belong to Christ. (Little Office of the Blessed Virgin Mary, Page 138, 1 Corinthians 15:22-23).

The other false teaching is what some of us have been taught that we have to wait till we physically die to go to heaven. This is what the great deceiver is known for, deceiving us and depriving us from heaven on earth in the here and now, and forever more. We can experience a new heaven and a new earth, when we go inside of ourselves, we can manifest the word of God in us the world. In the end when Jesus Christ comes for the living and the dead He comes in great glory and we can ascend to the Throne with and in Him, to the new heaven and new earth. And the dead can be resurrected from sleep and given life with and in Jesus Christ Crucified through God's Almighty Power and we can experience the new heaven and new earth which is symbolic of heaven on earth and we can be given everlasting life with and in Jesus Christ Crucified.

We can follow our Father's will and we can do what's right, just and lawful. Then we can find that the kingdom of God is within each of us in the world. Thy Kingdom come thy will be done on earth as it is in heaven. We are made of the earth, and heaven on earth can be manifested within us. We know that faith depends on hearing of the word, and we also know that good was to be expected from these that would come out of the purifying experience of the Babylonian exile to become the New Israel. This is what this exercise hopes to accomplish in Israel. Many books have been opened, and this scroll is presented to God's children that we might learn from instruction, turn from evil and our iniquities and live as the Lord lives: "A highway shall be there, and it shall be called the Holy Way; the unclean shall not travel on it, but it shall be for God's people; no traveler, not even fools, shall go astray. No lion shall be there, nor shall any ravenous beast come up on it; they shall not be found there, but the redeemed shall walk there. And the ransomed of the Lord shall return, and come to Zion with singing; everlasting joy shall be upon their heads; they shall obtain joy and gladness, and sorrow and sighing shall flee away." (Isaiah 35:8-10). That we as a whole might do God's will and live; as the Lord lives, that no one be left behind. (Left 4 dead). "Judge yourselves on what Christ is rather than what you are. Satan will try to spoil your peace by reminding you of your sinfulness and imperfection: you can only meet his accusations by faith fully holding to the Gospel and refusing to wear the yoke of slavery." (Spurgeon's evening by evening Page 264). Our Father is pure light; we are also light because of the Host that resides in us. We are a light to the world, a warning to those in darkness, we are pointing out every sin and what it leads to. In this way we are clear of the blood of all men. As long as creation continues to be faithful and fruitful as God the Father commanded He will live with us and in us. Our Father is the God of the Universe and He holds all things in His hands.

I would like to compliment my work and edify with what John Paul II wrote: "When the Council speaks of the eschatological character of the pilgrim Church it does so on the basis of this awareness. God, who is the just Judge, the Judge who rewards good and punishes evil, is none other than the God of Abraham, of Isaac, of Moses, and also of Christ, who is His Son. This God is, above all, Love. Not just Mercy, but Love. Not only the Father of the prodigal son, but the Father who "gave his only Son, so that everyone who believes in him might not perish but might have eternal life" (cf. Jn 3:16). This truth which the Gospel teaches about God requires a certain change in focus with regard to eschatology. First of all, eschatology is not what will take place in the future, something happening only after earthly life is finished. Eschatology has already begun with the coming of Christ. The ultimate eschatological event was His redemptive Death and His Resurrection. This is the beginning of "a new heaven and a new earth" (cf. Rev 21:1). For everyone, life beyond death is connected with the affirmation: "I believe in the resurrection of the body," and then: "I believe in the forgiveness of sins and in life everlasting." This is Christocentric eschatology. (His Holiness John Paul II: Crossing The Threshold of Hope page 177).

I would like for all to understand what it is that we believe pertaining to Mary being conceived without sin. God cannot abide in souls that are unclean, so in order for Mary or us to conceive the Holy Spirit, we have to be without sin. Mary was born without sin in order for her to give Jesus thus life to the world, and we are reborn without sin, this is the truth, other wise Jesus and God cannot come and live with and in us. We truly have to be cleansed mind, body, soul and spirit by Jesus Christ Crucified in God's Almighty Power through the Holy Spirit. "Mary occupies a place in the Church which is highest after Christ and yet very close to us for you chose her to give the world that very Life which renews all things, Jesus Christ, your Son and our Lord.

And so we praise you, Mary, virgin and mother. After the Savior himself, you alone are all holy, free from the stain of sin, gifted by God from the first instant of your conception with a unique holiness.

Mary, free from all sin and led by the Holy Spirit, you embraced God's saving will with a full heart, and devoted yourself totally as a handmaid of the Lord to the fulfillment of his will in your life, and to the mystery of our redemption.

Mary, your privileged and grace-filled origin is the Father's final step in preparing humanity to receive its Redeemer in human form.

Your fullness of grace is the Father's sign of his favor to the Church and also his promise to the Church of its perfection as the Bride of Christ, radiant in beauty.

Your holiness in the beginning of your life is the foreshadowing of that all-embracing holiness with which the Father will surround his people when his Son comes at the end of time to greet us." (Little Office of the Blessed Virgin Mary: Hymn Pages 61, 62). Help us by Mary's prayers to live with and in your presence without sin. We ask this through our Lord Jesus Christ, your Son, who lives and reigns with you and the Holy Spirit, one God, forever and ever. May the Lord bless us, protect us from evil and bring us to everlasting life, Amen. "The Lord, the ruler over the kings of the earth, will come; blessed are they who are ready to go and welcome him."(Divine Office Page 867).

When we go inside, mind, body, soul and spirit we can store our treasures in heaven within the City of God during our life time. We can experience heaven on earth through the exercise of God's Almighty Power with and in Jesus Christ Crucified in the unity of the Holy Spirit. When we hear of the saints interceding for the living and the dead, I believe this is when we are brought to our knees and we realize that those people that are living are living in heaven on earth in a state of grace, and they (the saints) although they are deceased, yet still living spiritually and physically are members of Jesus Christ body. This is why we acknowledge their spiritual and physical existence so that we the living and the dead may also learn to all live together in our spirituality in the new heaven and new earth. All of us the living and dead united as one as members of Jesus Christ's Glorified body living together through the Holy Spirit under Jesus Christ the Head. All of us one in Spirit, then all praise, glory and honor are given to the Father, Son and Holy Spirit. So in reality we are not praising and glorifying the saints or their bodies but rather we are praising and glorifying the body of God that they dwell in. We can fall in love with those in heaven because of their love, and faith in Jesus Christ. We can acknowledge their spiritual existence in the Trinity. And we can acknowledge that they and we are all one in the same body of Jesus Christ Crucified in the unity of the Holy Spirit. This spiritual and physical existence that we dwell in is precious and most holy. Jesus Christ had to suffer and die and be resurrected from the dead so that we could all live with and in the Father and the Son in the Unity of the Holy Spirit with everlasting life in the new heaven and new earth. And this is why we look forward to going to Mass so that our sweet Lord Jesus and our Father can feed the life within us with the Body and Blood of our Savior Jesus Christ through the Holy Spirit. And those of us living and those of us that are dead need the prayers of the saints and the exercise of God's Almighty Power and Jesus Christ Crucified in our lives, to bring restoration into our lives so we can be brought to everlasting life in the kingdom of God through the Holy Spirit in our mind, body, soul, and spirit in the here and now while we have time, and forever more. These prayers are powerful but only can be manifested through faith in Jesus Christ and with co-operation and free will from each person individually. Do not believe the lie and half truth of the great deceiver and miss out on the wonderful gift that Jesus is offering us, to live in the new heaven and new earth in the here and now, and forever more, with those that are dwelling with and in Jesus Christ in heaven on earth.

"God Himself will set me free, from the hunter's snare. That is from those who would trap me with lying words. (Divine Office page 278). Thank you dear sweet, kind and loving Father for your concern pertaining to us, that we would find the way, the truth and life in your Word through the Holy Spirit.

Our Sweetest Mother Mary has been misunderstood for so long. By faith and virtue of Mary's life with Jesus Christ we can understand some of her sorrow and her joy. We really need to take a closer LOOK into her heart and see all that she represents.

Adam and Eve brought disobedience, unfaithfulness and sin and death to us. Jesus and Mary bring faith, obedience and life everlasting through the New Covenant which is world without end. Where Jesus is you should also find Mary.

So we need to understand how important it is to behold them both in our hearts and consecrate our life to them in order to move forward in the love of God.

Our Father Commands us to honor our Father and Mother. When we do Our Father's will He is pleased and those that are found being faithful children are great in heaven and on earth. The two places that we find our Joy is in God's providence. (Heaven and Earth). He loves us because we are his children, and we are made of the earth and His Spirit. He wants to share all things with us. The fruit from our Mother Mary is so sweet and good. Some of her children are actually dying from starvation. Our Mother Mary is yearning for her children to be feed.

My desire is to use the exercise of God's Almighty Power and Jesus Christ Crucified through the Holy Spirit and to exercise you the world: To drive out the evil from the people of God. To expel the false teaching that is in the world.

All fall short of the glory of God. Because of our erroneous ways, we are partially blinded to the Truth and the Promises of Christ.

And some of us are also dull in the senses due to our selfish behavior which is due to the old man {anti-Christ}.

As long as we dwell in the old world we will continue to fall short of God's glory. Only through the baptism of water and the spirit of Fire that destroys the old world spiritually and physically can we receive our new spiritual body which is Jesus Christ' glorified body, in the new heaven and new earth. Only then can we give Our Father His glory. Our glorified body is a gift from Jesus Christ. We share in His glory, not ours. The Lord sees us in every age. That is why he came 2010 years ago to destroy what stops us from being with Him: Then, now and in the future. Jesus Christ gives us the ability to dwell with and in Him in Heavenly places spiritually and physically if we follow Him in this life, once the old world has passed by fire, world without end, Amen. The new heaven and new earth can come down from heaven spiritually and physically and we can become Jesus Christ's Bride's and all this can happen to us before we fall asleep in the Lord and are pronounced dead in the here and now. The first step is to become aware that God can save us through

His Son and our free will, but He needs our co-operation, He needs our undivided attention, total sincerity. The First commandment is to love God with all your heart, mind, and soul. The Second commandment is to love your neighbor as yourself. (To serve and to love your brothers and sisters as I have loved you).

Jesus Christ Conquered Death so we don't have to wait till we fall asleep in death for His Promises to be fulfilled. We the living can posses Jesus and we can move forward in heaven on earth. And when we fall asleep and we are pronounced dead, yet our spirit is still living in the Lord. We know we are still living; being physically dead does not destroy our spiritual life or our relationship with or in the Trinity. We can realize that our spiritual life has no end, because we are made in God's image. "Sun of Justice, the Immaculate Virgin Mary was the white dawn announcing your rising; grant that we may always live in the light of your coming." (Little Office of the Blessed Virgin Mary Page 41).

"Father, you prepared the Virgin Mary to be the worthy mother of your Son. You let her share beforehand in the salvation Christ would bring by his death, and kept her sinless from the first moment of her conception. Help us by her prayers to live in your presence without sin. We ask through our Lord Jesus Christ, you're Son, who lives, and reigns with you and the Holy Spirit, one God, for ever and ever." (Little Office of the Blessed Virgin Mary: page 42).

Our Father's promises have been and always will be attainable. They are there by virtue of His word, and can be manifested by Faith in Jesus Christ, through Him, with Him, in Him in the Unity of the Holy Spirit, all glory and honor are yours Almighty father for ever and ever. This is the way to our Father, when those that do His will live spiritually and physically in the here and now and forever more.

We have to acknowledge we have been in error, and correct our ways in order to see and hear perfectly, and be perfect. He is commanding us to be like Him. Jesus told us everything God gave Him, and this he gives to us. Jesus Christ is perfect and God is calling us also to be perfect with and in the Trinity + mind, body, soul and spirit.

Thy kingdom come thy will be done on earth as it is in heaven. We know that in the Book of Revelations John talks about a woman clothed with the sun, and that she becomes pregnant with a male child which is Jesus. So we say: "Yes, come Lord Jesus" and we conceive in our mind body soul and spirit. We will be in Travail with the child Jesus. The Beast wants to kill us and the baby. God puts us in a safe place. Spiritually we bring forth the child that would be Jesus in us. "We say:" Through Him + mind, with Him + body, in Him + in the soul, + in the Unity of the Holy Spirit all Honor and Glory is yours Almighty Father forever and ever, Amen. It is our job to raise Jesus up within us individually with and in the word of God through the Holy Spirit in God's Almighty Power.

We know a lot about Christ and what He taught. But let's go back to Babylon, that ancient city. The definition of Babylon is any city or place of great wealth, luxury, and vice. It is a form of our spiritual captivity.

"This rather, is the fasting that I wish: Releasing those bound unjustly... Sharing your bread with the hungry...Clothing the naked when you see them." (Isaiah 58:6-7).

We the exiles through the Holy Spirit are going to travel back in time to Babylon we are going to acknowledge our sins. Then God calls us out of her for He is going to destroy that city. We travel to Jerusalem, and ask God to forgive us our sins and we will die with Jesus Christ and we are going to ask for Mary's Intercession, that through her loving hands she will hand us to her Son, that He would send the Baptism of Fire upon us the world, that we would be purified by the spirit of fire, thus Jesus and Mary could present us to our Father blameless and prepared to enter into the kingdom of God in heaven on earth.

We are going to be fasting and we are going to be traveling at the speed of light. No longer are we completely limited by time and space we can move freely with Jesus Christ in the Holy Spirit through God's Almighty Power. We the living can travel back in time to our spiritual captivity which is called Babylon and we can call on Almighty God to draw the remaining people out of darkness that are living, so that no one is left 4 dead. God our Father promises no one has to be left behind. I believe our Lord is expecting us. We can return to Babylon by tearing a hole in the wall (which is the scriptures) and we can experience our sins there and our repentant heart can lead us to Jerusalem and we can die to sin at the foot of Jesus Christ' Cross, with Jesus and Mary through much grief, which leads to sincere repentance by the sword, which is the Word of God, with Jesus Christ Crucified and with Holy Mary in God's Almighty power. Thus we have seen the destruction of Jerusalem. At that point with God's grace our Maker will rebuild the walls of Jerusalem with Jesus Christ Crucified through the Holy Spirit. Jesus Christ being the Chief Stone rejected by us the builders is now being offered again. Now we the unbelievers and sinners have accepted, we do believe in Jesus Christ and in God the Father, also in His Almighty Power, and we the land of God are the living stones that will be put atop of the12 foundations of the 12 Apostles, the Prophets and with Jesus Christ being the corner stone. "You are strangers and aliens no longer, No, you are fellow citizens of the saints and members of the household of God. You form a building which rises on the foundation of the apostles and prophets, with

Christ Jesus himself as the capstone. Through him the whole structure is fitted together and takes shape as a holy temple in the Lord; in him you are being built into this temple, to become a dwelling place for God in the Spirit." (Ephesians 2:19-20). "On the foundation stones of the heavenly Jerusalem, the names of the twelve apostles of the Lamb are written; the Lamb of God is the light of that holy City (Alleluia)." (Divine Office Page: 1393). Thus the walls of Jerusalem are rebuilt by God our Maker. We have made individual retribution for our sins. That we may become a new creation in Christ Jesus (regenerated). That we may inherit our land as God the Father promised. That no one be left behind (left 4 dead). Through this exercise God is found, we are found and He is being faithful and true, we the unbelievers and sinners have truly repented and have turned from our evil ways and have been given mercy, justice and love by our Savior Jesus Christ all in God's Almighty Power through the Holy Spirit. We can bring our spiritual captivity to where Christ is in Jerusalem. Jews and Christians have died to sin at the foot of the cross and experienced spiritual death with Jesus and Mary with broken hearts. And through Jesus Christ Crucified and the exercise of Almighty Power through the Holy Spirit we have also died by the sword. Jesus Christ's Mother was also pierced by the sword. We have been restored to our natural state, we the living can no longer eternally die, no death in us, all sin has been removed; now we can conceive the Holy Spirit without sin. I am talking about all sin that has kept people from entering into glory in the new heaven and new earth. We have been given Freedom and Liberty to enter the new heaven and new earth through Jesus Christ Crucified and the exercise of God's Almighty Power through the Holy Spirit.

No sin remains in us after we die to sin and experience spiritual death with and in our Lord and Savior Jesus Christ Crucified, through our heavenly Fathers Almighty Power. And because we the living conceived the Holy Spirit without sin (we the living are reborn with an immaculate conception) like Mary. We remain a virgin spiritually. We have experienced justification through the justice of God and our Savior Jesus Christ through the Holy Spirit. Our repentant heart moves us forward in God's love and divine care. While we are there at Jesus' Crucifixion we can ask God for His divine mercy, forgive us Father for we have sinned against God and man. We have free will and we can accept the gift of Redemption we can die to sin and be resurrected from the grave through spiritual death with Jesus Christ' death through the exercise of God's Almighty Power. And we can unite as one with and in Jesus Christ's Glorified Body and we can be given a new spiritual life with and in Jesus Christ' body, and in this way we can become the members of His Holy body to live in the new heaven and new earth with and in Jesus Christ spiritually and physically and this is what we call Heaven on Earth. We have been given the Way the Truth and Life, we have been resurrected from the grave through the spirit with and in Jesus Christ Crucified through our Fathers Almighty Power. We have become the members of a pure spiritual body that of Jesus'. Are not angel's spirits also? Has God in His great love created angels? Do not angels dwell with God? We are no longer carrying sin and death that we inherited from Adam and Eve that barred us from heaven on earth. Rather no longer are we able to eternally die, and because of the way we conceived the Word of God through the Holy Spirit we also remain a virgin just like our Mother Mary, only ours is spiritual and in this way we are manifesting our Lord, just like Mary Jesus Christ's Mother, only she literally gave birth to God in the Flesh. We do it spiritually, as Mary, Jesus Christ's Mother also conceived spiritually. We can be found being faithful and true, lawful and doing what is right, and we shall surely live. Do not angels also live forever? We shall not die. We have obtained the promise of God which is peace, eternal happiness and everlasting life in the new heaven and new earth with and in Jesus Christ. Israel can become the New Israel.

Once we the living have said: "yes," come Lord Jesus" and we have truly repented of our evil ways, of our own free will and have turned to God for help from Jesus. Jesus can save us from ourselves, and Jesus can deliver us from the evil within us individually through God's Almighty Power and our cooperation. We can make individual retribution for our sins, although there could still be temporal punishment due to justice. Once our sins and our lives have been sacrificed with and in Jesus Christ on the cross, we are dead. He sends the Spirit of Fire upon us the world. That fire can consume and destroy all the root of evil in us individually, and we are purified by that same fire, we can be resurrected from spiritual death to a new spiritual life with and in Jesus Christ's Body. If we reject Jesus Christ we experience judgment, we can accept and believe in Jesus Christ and be forgiven and we can receive Divine Mercy. Our hearts can be set on fire by the word of God, and we can be purified which leads to a state of grace which is called pure, clean from the inside out. We can receive an Immaculate Heart. We can be given the new pure root that of (Mary) from the tree of life and knowledge (God) that produces the vine (Jesus) the vine produces the branches that would be us, that we could live with and in them in the garden in heaven on earth. That the Garden of Eden is within each of us, thus all around everywhere you look. The fullness of Christ's grace can reside in us, in the here and now, and forevermore through the exercise of God's Almighty Power and Jesus Christ Crucified through the Holy Spirit, which consumes and destroys sin and death in us, and gives us everlasting life, and the fullness of grace and truth.

No longer are we able to eternally die, we have become perfect and have done the will of God. And this is good in God's eyes. We are living in time and space with God's children, praising and glorifying God world without end. All this is how we can live in the Holy Spirit and become holy. We are called to be holy like our Savior Jesus Christ in heaven.

When these things are taking place, we can see Jews and the Christians coming together, and the will of God being done in each generation, and we can know that the first resurrection has come upon us because the beast-Satan, anti-Christ, the dragon has been chained up for a thousand years. The second death and resurrection occurs when death is hurled into the pool of fire. This is why Jesus Christ died on the Cross so that all His children would come to the truth, no more eternal death. "God so loved the world that He gave His only begotten Son that everyone who believes in Him should not perish, but should have eternal life." (John 3:16). That we the living and the dead could be where He is at all times. We can come to peace with God, and we can live as one with and in Jesus Christ, drawing from the Tree of Life and of Knowledge from the Garden of Eden, where all the saved and redeemed are glorifying our Father and Son through the Holy Spirit. We can be made worthy and we the living and the dead can be in communion with the Martyrs, Saints and Angels that have suffered and died throughout history through the Holy Spirit with and in Jesus Christ Crucified, through God's Almighty Power. When we allow the Trinity to do its work in our hearts and our lives; our mind body and soul and spirit can be restored to its natural state like it was in the beginning. We the living and the dead can be united as one in the spirit and one in the body as members of Jesus Christ's Holy body through the Holy Spirit, in God's Almighty Power.

"We beg you not to receive the grace of God in vain, for He says, "In an acceptable time I have heard you; on a day of salvation I have helped you". Now is the acceptable time. Now is the day of salvation." (Divine Office page 266). "2 Corinthians 6:1-4a".

"In a time of favor I answer you, on the day of salvation I help you, to restore the land and allot the desolate heritages, saying to the prisoners: Come out! To those in darkness: Show yourselves! Along the ways they shall find pasture, on every bare height shall their pastures be. They shall not hunger or thirst, nor shall the scorching wind or the sun strike them; for he who pities them leads them and guides them beside springs of water." (Divine Office page 188 Isaiah 49:8-10).

promises of Jesus Christ; we the living and the dead have been delivered from evil and we have been redeemed by our savior Jesus Christ with His precious blood.

Jesus Christ is with us always whether living or dead. We are living in Jesus Christ's body we are the members of His body, and we like Him can never die. We can rejoice in the Truth and dance and sing the hymn of Moses and of the Lamb. Jesus Christ has opened all the seals pertaining to the Book of Revelation. Jesus Christ is the one that is Worthy. With Jesus in time and space we have been given Freedom and Liberty to be called Children of the Light, we are His adopted children. We are also the children of the promise. We can give birth to Jesus Christ in us and Jesus Christ can grow up in us and Jesus can destroy the root of evil in us. Jesus Christ has shown us the way to live with Him and in Him in the new heaven and new earth which is heaven on earth. Rejoice in the Lord, our King has come, through the Holy Spirit into our hearts and into our lives to live with and in us, that we would reign with and in Jesus forever and ever. "I rejoice heartily in the Lord, in my God is the joy of my soul; for he has clothed me with a robe of salvation; and wrapped me in a mantel of justice, like a bride bedecked with her jewels." (Isaiah 61:10).

Are not the people being delivered from evil those being set in stone, to be living stones unto the Lord? That our faith: may never faultier, and give way to concupiscence. This knowing of knowledge gives us; the people delivered and redeemed the land of promise. We have become solid as a rock through Jesus Christ Crucified in God's Almighty Power, through the Holy Spirit. Let all the earth rejoice in its new splendor. Praise God the Father, Son and Holy Spirit, with unending joy. That we the world would find trueness of life from the earth that we were made from through the Holy Spirit with God's Almighty Power in Jesus Christ Crucified. "I saw before me a huge crowd which no one could count from every nation and race, people and tongue. They stood before the throne and the Lamb, dressed in long white robes and holding palm branches in their hands. They cried out in a loud voice, "Salvation is from our God, who is seated on the throne, and from the Lamb!" All the angels who were standing around the throne and the elders and the four living creatures fell down before the throne to worship God. They said: "Amen! Praise and glory, wisdom and thanksgiving and honor, power and might, to our God forever and ever. Amen!" (Revelation 7:9-12). Not my way, but your way Father: teach us your ways through your Son and Holy Spirit, that wisdom and love may guide us all the days of our lives. Our Father who art in heaven hallowed be thy name, thy kingdom come thy will be done, on earth as it is in heaven, give us this day our daily bread and forgive us our trespasses as we forgive those who trespass against us, and lead us not into temptation but deliver us from evil, Amen.

"By your birth you destroyed the chains of death; free the dead from all their chains." (Divine Office page194).

"May your birth bring joy to the world. Sanctify us Heavenly Father and bring us to everlasting life in Jesus Christ name, Amen." (Divine Office page:194).

"Liberator of mankind, through the Virgin Mary you came to renew us, through her intercession keep us from our old ways."(Divine Office page 194).

"There is no condemnation now for those who are in Christ Jesus. The law of the spirit, the spirit of life in Christ Jesus, has freed you from the law of sin and death. The law was powerless because of its weakening by the flesh. Then God sent his Son in the likeness of sinful flesh as a sin offering, thereby condemning sin in the flesh, so that the just demands of the law might be fulfilled in us who live, not according to the flesh, but according to the spirit. Those who live according to the flesh are intent on the things of the flesh, those who live according to the spirit, on those of the spirit." (Divine Office page 196 Romans 8:1-5). Through Him with Him in Him in the Unity of the Holy Spirit all Glory and Honor is yours Almighty Father for ever and ever, Amen. Blessed are you who do the Will of My Father. Those that do the will of my Father are His mother, brother, and sister. So like Mary the Mother of God we are also called to be His family members in time and space. We are to become obedient at all times doing our Fathers will, in order to give the light to those still in darkness. We can be bright so bright that all that is done in secret is brought to light, so that the souls that are lost can find Jesus Christ, and those that have been waiting for the fullness of time may come into His Presence and enjoy their life with and in Jesus Christ. And we can share with our brothers and sisters everything that God has given us. Oh what rejoicing there is in heaven, when all God's children can see and hear again. The Jews were not the only ones blinded. We were also blinded.

The hearer that has received justice and mercy, thus righteousness who can see and hear, is to put on clothing of goodwill to serve God, and to do His will, so that all can see Christ in each of us. Through God's Almighty Power those that are stuck in purgatory or doing nothing in limbo will see Christ in us and they can follow the light that is within us. And we can take them in the Spirit to Jesus Christ Crucified through God's Almighty Power. I am using the term limbo for those of us that are spiritually dead, that haven't come to life with and in Jesus thus ascending to the Thorne with and in Jesus in His great glory. Limbo is a location between Heaven and Hell; it applies to the living and the dead. No longer will there be false teaching. We can lead them in the spirit to the Truth in Jesus Christ Crucified through the exercise of God's Almighty Power. This is for what the saints have been interceding for throughout Eternity. Jesus Christ, Mary, Apostles, and all the angels and saints have and are a beacon for us. But some people have been under false teaching, which blinded them from seeing our lights. They thought the saints were idols. Far from it.

The pitchfork can be thrown into the lake of fire along with the beast that is in us, and we can move without the prodding of the devils fork, which produced lies, and destructive behavior, torment, lack of all that is Good. It know longer has a hold on us. Christ has repossessed us in time and space. The pitchfork is symbolic of our slavery.

It is time to go to the wedding feast; our Bridegroom awaits us with joy unknown. We can have every need met; Jesus Christ has a place prepared for us, His bride's. And all that enter into Marriage with Christ are doing the Will of God. This is the Beatific Vision where Christ says thy Will be done on Earth as it is in Heaven.

We can live by faith and grace and from the Body and Blood of Jesus Christ, and from the Waters that flow freely from Him. And we can live with and in the presence of Jesus Christ, because He is every where you LOOK and He truly does live with us and in us, and He loves us so much.

I know that the word of God is alive. God the Father and His Son Jesus Christ truly do dwell among us. And also through us, through the Holy Spirit here in heaven on earth. And we the living and the dead will be so amazed when we can see our loved ones in heaven on earth with us. Can you imagine seeing all the Holy Ones, and the Holy Family? Death no longer separates those living and those dead. We come to you Father through the Holy Spirit with Mary and with your Son in thanksgiving for all our spiritual gifts. You have filled our hearts with your cornucopia of love; all our needs have been met.

We are being made worthy by our Savior Jesus Christ. Not by any thing we have done. If we say "yes, come Lord Jesus" and merely co-operate with God's divine plan of salvation, we can give all honor and glory to the Trinity through the Holy Spirit. Otherwise we are still in darkness. We can be true and faithful to our lover and we can say "yes, come Lord Jesus." The romance can begin. The Bible is truly a love story and it can become a reality with and in us.

To live in Heaven is "to be with Christ." The elect "live in Christ," but they retain, or rather find, their true identity, and their own name. For life is to be with Christ, where Christ is, there is life, there is the kingdom. (CCC. #1025). This fulfills The Two Commandments of Christ. The old world (Israel) is passing away to the spiritual life with and in Jesus and we can leave all things behind to follow Jesus Christ: Through Him, with Him, in Him in the Unity of the Holy Spirit all Glory and Honor is yours Almighty Father forever and ever, Amen: This is what we call the New Israel. In the end when Jesus comes into our hearts and our lives it's personal, and if He reveals Himself to you it is through the Holy Spirit, visions, dream, manifestation what ever means He wishes, we have no control over these things and it is done in God's Almighty Power, not ours. There is Jesus there is the kingdom. We also have to remember that He is half human and half divine so we know that He Himself lives forever in heaven, with His family.

I highly recommend going to a Catholic bookstore and buying the large print of the Divine Office and join the choirs of angels praising and glorifying our Lord all around the world every minute of the day. It is an honor to be part of those that are doing God's will. There is much more to be said about all that is good. We will find it in the Divine Office and in the Little Office of the Blessed Virgin Mary. "Our Father is asking us to establish a feast and office in His honor, under the title of Father of all mankind." I am quoting from (The Father Speaks to His Children written by Mother Eugenia). I am hoping and praying it will happen soon. We are citizens of the earth and we can ask to be made citizens of Heaven on earth. Heaven on Earth is a gift from God and His Son Jesus Christ and it is given to us through the Holy Spirit. Help us always Father, so that we can follow your commands.

"Declare your sins to one another, and pray for one another, that you may find healing.

The fervent petition of a holy man is powerful indeed. My brothers, the case may arise among you of someone straying from the truth, and of another bringing him back. Remember this: the person who brings a sinner back from his way will save his soul from death and cancel a multitude of sins."(James 5:16, 19-20).

"Grant that Christians, as your Prophets, may make you known in every place, and bear witness to you with living faith and hope and love. Give your strength to all in distress, and help us to raise them up through our loving concern. Teach the faithful to

See your power to save. Author of life, remember those who have passed from this world, grant them the Glory of your risen life." "Your word is the Lantern to light our way. Alleluia." (Divine Office page 382 and 383).

"New City of Zion, let your heart sing for joy, see how humbly your King comes to save you." (Divine Office page 64).

"The law was given to Moses, but grace and truth come through Jesus Christ." (Divine Office page 64).

"Humbly yet confidently, let us invoke Christ the Lord whose favor has been shown to all people: Lord have mercy. Christ, born of the Father before the ages, splendor of his glory, image of his being, your word holds all creation in being, - we ask you to give new life to our world through your gospel. Christ, you were born into the world at the fullness of time to save mankind and to give freedom to every creature, - we ask you to extend the liberty of our sonship in you to all people.

Christ, consubstantial Son of the Father, begotten before the dawn of day, and born in Bethlehem in fulfillment of the Scriptures, - we ask you to make your Church a notable example of poverty and simplicity. Christ, God and Man, Lord of David and Son of David, fulfillment of all prophecies, - we pray that Israel may recognize you as its Messiah." (Divine Office page 172).

NOTE: The words Second Coming, Coming of Christ and gathering of the redeemed are simultaneous. Jesus Christ, Messiah and Redeemer are synonymous.

NOTE: Regarding tense in the message, and its purposeful meaning: Past, Present Tense, and Future. The message is without tense of the Second Coming of Christ, the time is not apparent. Only God knows the time. "Just as in Adam all die, so too in Christ shall all be brought to life, but each one in proper order. Christ the first fruits, then, at his coming, those who belong to Christ." (Little Office of the Blessed Virgin Mary: page 138. 1 Corinthians 15:22-23).

"Blinded, couldn't get a hold to understand-See, I am doing something new! Now it springs forth, do you not perceive it?" (Isaiah: 43-19).

"This is the old world and the Beginning of the New. The first resurrection happened in the tomb of Jesus Christ and the second resurrection began shortly there after and will continue till the end of time." (Billy Easley my husband).

Some of Gods people in Ancient times and when Christ was alive and even now have been waiting for His coming, because they were and are LOOKING for the wrong type of Messiah. They were LOOKING for someone to save them from their enemies, not the true enemy, which is the great deceiver that leads everyone to Hell.

Christ is still offering a better way which is the Truth: Everlasting life to those who would accept and believe in him. Christ can conquer the Beast which resides in each of us, and that Beast can be chained up for a thousand years. The second death and resurrection doesn't hurt us at all. We haven't fallen asleep in physical death yet. We can be truly repentant of all our evil ways and we can turn to God and seek Jesus, thus be given life with and in the Trinity and then be pleasing to God.

We can fall down on our knees in true repentance and ask Our Lord for His divine mercy and we know we are forgiven because Christ was crucified for that very purpose. By virtue of Jesus Christ Crucified, we can experience death to sin with and in Jesus Christ through the Holy Spirit Spiritually and physically through God's Almighty Power. Jesus Christ Crucified through God's Almighty Power destroyed death and all sin in us. We can accept Jesus Christ gift of Salvation that He offers from the cross. We can pass judgment and know that every sin we have committed has been forgiven. Oh! What Joy we have in our hearts.

So now we have been justified by faith in deeds done with and in our Savior and Lord Jesus Christ. In His merits; not our own. That's why he had to die for sin, because we the world could not save ourselves. We can be purified, when the Baptism of Fire sets us the world on Fire or we can be in purgatory waiting to be purified, the fire can consume all our sinful roots. And this can happen like a thief in the night, it pretty much happens and we don't even know when it happened. All the old ways the old man the deceiver every thing false can be destroyed by the Baptism of Fire, in the twinkling of the eye. I know because I received the baptism of Fire, and I was purified. The chains of sin and death were destroyed by Jesus Christ in God's Almighty Power through the Holy Spirit. The old world was destroyed by fire and the new heaven and new earth came down from heaven by the grace of our Lord and Savior Jesus Christ, through the Holy Spirit in the Power of God the Father.

We the living can allow the fire of baptism to destroy our old ways that we might be resurrected from the grave, with a new heart and a new clean spirit to live with and in our Lord and Savior Jesus Christ in the unity of the Holy Spirit. We can allow the new heaven and new earth and the gifts given to us from Jesus, to come down from our Father from heaven through the Holy Spirit. That we all be one with and in Jesus in heaven on earth, with God and all His family in the here and now, and forever more through the Holy Spirit in God's Almighty Power. We can accept this precious and most holy gift from our Lord Jesus Christ. Now we have become justified and sanctified. Redeemed free from sin and death we have been made Holy through Him, with Him, in Him, in the Unity of the Holy Spirit, all Glory and Honor is Yours Almighty Father forever and ever. Amen.

We can experience Jesus Christ's pain but it will not harm us. Our heart can grow and grow. We can also fill our Mother Mary's sorrow her pain her grief and the sword that pierced her heart. We can also feel the pain of all those that have died or suffered in the name of Jesus Christ that have done His Will. There is no way we can actually fill their pain, but we can relate somewhat, our heart's at this moment should feel broken, and our broken heart should tell us we can lighten the load of the cross, by becoming obedient to our Fathers Word. Then it can dawn on us what He has done for us. Jesus Christ has redeemed the world. All Glory and Honor to you dear sweet Jesus. We have to put on the Armor of Jesus Christ Crucified with God's Almighty Power and guard ourselves against the enemy that is still roaming the earth.

"Mary, Mother of God, we salute you. Precious vessel, worthy of the whole world's reverence, you are an ever-shining light, the crown of virginity, the symbol of orthodoxy, an indestructible temple, the place that held him whom no place can contain, mother and virgin. Because of you the holy gospels could say: Blessed is he who comes in the name of the Lord.

We salute you, for in your holy womb he, who is beyond all limitation, was confined. Because of you the holy Trinity is glorified and adored; the cross is called precious and is venerated throughout the world; the heavens exult; the angels and archangels make merry; demons are put to flight; the devil, that tempter, is thrust down from heaven; the fallen race of man is taken up on high; all creatures possessed by the madness of idolatry have attained knowledge of the truth; believers receive holy baptism; the oil of gladness is poured out; the Church is established throughout the world; pagans are brought to repentance.

What more is there to say? Because of you the light of the only-begotten Son of God has shone upon those who sat in darkness and in the shadow of death; prophets pronounced the word of God; the apostles preached salvation to the Gentiles; the dead are raised to life, and kings rule by the power of the holy Trinity." (From a homily delivered at the Council of Ephesus by Saint Cyril of Alexandria, Bishop (Hom. 4: PG 77, 991,995-996) Divine Office pages 47 and 48).

"O Key of David, O royal Power of Israel controlling at your will the gate of heaven: come, break down the prison walls of death for those who dwell in darkness and the shadow of death; and lead your captive people into freedom." (Divine Office page 1217).

When we celebrate Jesus Christ' memorial at Mass we are united as one in the Holy Spirit of God through Jesus Christ Crucified with God's Almighty Power and we, though many are one in the spirit of Jesus Christ. We the living that believe we have experienced spiritual death with Jesus Christ' death, and that we have been resurrected from the grave with and in Jesus Christ through the Holy Spirit can dwell in Heaven on earth with and in Him, and with Holy Mary, Joseph the Martyrs and all the Saints and Angels forever and ever. Now and forevermore we can be made Worthy to receive the Body and Blood of our Lord Jesus Christ. We have been regenerated, all of us one with and in Jesus Christ Glorifying God world without end, Amen.

We have been set Free by the Word of God and Jesus Christ Crucified through the Holy Spirit and the exercise of God's Almighty Power to be His Universal Church. We have witnessed to the Truth of Free Will and our Spiritual Death with and in Jesus Christ Crucified, through God's Almighty Power. Our faith in the promises of Christ can be manifested in us and we can receive the new heaven and new earth promised by Almighty Father. We have inherited our Land, which is the new heaven and the new earth come down from Our Father, we can be His Church the Body of Christ, we can become His Bride, and we can live with Him and in Him forever and ever, Amen..

And this is what is celebrated every time Mass is offered all around the world. When Jesus is lifted up He is able to send the spirit to those who believe in Him. That we may unite as one in His spirit and in His body and we are one in His glory to God the Father. We fulfill Jesus Christ commandment at the last supper when He told the Apostles to do this in memory of me. We offer up to God the Father through the Holy Spirit the sacrifice of Jesus Christ's Crucifixion in God's Almighty Power, not ours, we offer up our spiritual death along with Jesus Christ's death. We also acknowledge Jesus' new life in the spirit that we may unite in newness of life with and in the spirit also. Along with these many blessings we offer our thankful hearts, in union with Mary's the Mother of God that we your children might always be pleasing and obedient to your word. By doing our Fathers will we are capable of pleasing Him.

The Word of God is alive, and God's Word lives forever. And we unite as one in faith in Jesus Christ through the Holy Spirit to receive such a great blessing, the ultimate fulfillment in the Beatific Vision. We are fed on the Body and Blood our Lord Jesus Christ which feeds the life within us. We the exiles have truly passed through time and space from the Cosmos at the speed of light to become spiritual beings to live spiritual lives and to live and love forever with and in Jesus Christ and with those we love on earth and in heaven forever and ever. We are God's people, Jesus Christ sets us free. And in each generation we are to be regenerated and consecrated to Jesus Christ and Mary through the Holy Spirit in God's Almighty Power in order to stay in a state of grace only offered through Jesus Christ. The only way to stay united with our Father at all times is when we are living through the Holy Spirit with and in Jesus Christ as members of His Crucified and His Glorified body. Whether our state of life is death or life it is in heaven on earth, it is all one, living and loving forever in Jesus Christ, through the Holy Spirit and in our Father's Almighty Power. And when the here and now is over and we fall asleep in Jesus Christ's friendship we know we are still united as one with and in Jesus Christ and that death cannot separate the unity of life that we share in Jesus Christ. I believe when our time ends, and our physical bodies are wore out our mind, soul and spirit, remain united with our Lord and God, to be reunited with our bodies in the resurrection.

In this way you can see that we the members of Jesus Christ's body can no longer eternally die whether we are dead or if we are alive. So in this way when people say you have to physically die before you can go to Heaven, you can tell them yes, and I did die at the foot of the cross, and we the people that live in the spirit live forever, that physical death does not separate God's kingdom. We of the spirit do not live according to the flesh or the world's point of view. But we need to remember our God is Spirit and Truth, and when Jesus comes He brings life everlasting in Heaven on earth, through the Holy Spirit in God's Almighty Power in the here and now, and also after physical death, forever more. We in the spirit are never separated from God and the things of heaven, by physical death. I believe our Lord and God gave us the ability to dwell with all those that live in heaven on earth whether we are awake or asleep in the Lord. Because of Jesus Christ's great sacrifice of His death, He has given us His love, His death, His life, and His kingdom and His truth, all through God's Almighty Power and given to us through the Holy Spirit. We have been made in God's image, that we may reflect His light to the world, that where there is darkness we would give light. In God's kingdom there is no darkness. The splendor of the unity of the spirit that we dwell in illuminates the earth through the Trinity.

We the dead and the living through the Holy Spirit have been exercised through God's Almighty Power and Jesus Christ Crucified and we have been made capable of running the race and being victorious in Jesus Christ Crucified. Through God's Almighty Power all things are possible, and we can win the Crown of Glory that Our Sweet Lord Jesus is offering us. Let us not be content unless we reflect the grace that is in Jesus Christ Crucified, and let our Mother Mary's soul be in each of us, that we can be reborn and or born again without sin. The life of Jesus Christ Crucified is the perfect example of virtue. So follow Jesus Christ Crucified to also become perfect in virtue.

"Breathe on me, breath of God, Fill me with life anew, that I may love the things you love, and do what you would do. Breathe on me, breath of God, until my heart is pure, until with you I have one will, to live and to endure. Breathe on me, breath of God, My soul with grace refine, until this earthly part of me Glows with your fire divine. Breathe on me, breath of God, so I shall never die, but live with you the perfect life in your eternity."(Little Office of the Blessed Virgin Mary page 157).

"Christ is the world's Light, he and none other; Born in our darkness, he became our brother. If we have seen him, we have seen the Father: Glory to God on high. Christ is the world's Peace, he and none other; No man can serve him and despise his brother. Who else unites us, one in God the Father? Glory to God on High.

Christ is the world's life, he and none other; Sold, once for silver, murdered here, our brother. He, who redeems us, reigns with God the Father: Glory to God on high. Give God the glory, God and none other; Give God the glory, Spirit, Son and Father; Give God the glory, God in man my brother; Glory to God on high." (Divine Office page.1514 Song 17

"The one whom the Father has sent into our hearts, the Spirit of his Son, is truly God. Consubstantial with the Father and the Son, the Spirit is inseparable from them, in both the inner life of the Trinity and his gift of love for the world. In adoring the Holy Trinity, life-giving, consubstantial, and indivisible, the Church's faith also professes the distinction of persons. When the Father sends his Word, he always sends his Breath. In their joint mission, the Son and the Holy Spirit are distinct but inseparable. To be sure, it is Christ who is seen, the visible image of the invisible God, but it is the Spirit who reveals him.

Jesus is Christ, "anointed," because the Spirit is his anointing, and everything that occurs from the Incarnation on derives from this fullness. When Christ is finally glorified, he can in turn send the Spirit from his place with the Father to those who believe in him: he communicates to them his glory, that is, the Holy Spirit who glorifies him.

From that time on, this joint mission is manifested in the children adopted by the Father in the Body of his Son: the mission of the Spirit of adoption is to unite them to Christ and make them live in him

The notion of anointing suggests … that there is no distance between the Son and the Spirit. Indeed, just as between the surface of the body and the anointing with oil neither reason nor sensation recognizes any intermediary, so the contact with the Son by faith must simultaneously first encounter the oil by contact.

In fact there is no part that is not covered by the Holy Spirit. That is why the confession of the Son's Lordship is made in the Holy Spirit by those who receive Him, the Spirit coming from all sides to those who approach the Son in Faith." (CCC, #689 and #690).

"Father, we ask you to give us victory and peace. In Jesus Christ, our Lord and King, we are already seated at your right hand. We look forward to praising you in the fellowship of all your saints in our heavenly homeland. The earth is shaken to its depths before the glory of your face." (Divine Office page 713)

All things can be ours, and we can live forever with and in Jesus Christ as the members of His body and we can ascend to the Throne with and in our Lord and Savior Jesus Christ Crucified in Our Father's Almighty Power. Alleluia, Alleluia, Alleluia.

In our mind, body, soul and spirit through Jesus Christ Crucified with and in the Holy Spirit, God has poured out the Way, Truth, and Life. We have received the Way, Truth and Life and we will continue to live with and in thee and in your love through the Holy Spirit knowing that you Lord are always there whether we are dead or alive it is all in your loving hands heavenly Father. Thank you, Father, Son and Holy Spirit for your unending patience.

"Be patient, my brothers, until the coming of the Lord. See how the farmer awaits the precious yield of the soil. He looks forward to it patiently while the soil receives the winter and the spring rains. You, too, must be patient. Steady your hearts, because the coming of the Lord is at hand. Do not grumble against one another, my brothers, lest you be condemned. See! The judge stands at the gate. As your models in suffering hardships and in patience, brothers, take the prophets who spoke in the name of the Lord. Those who have endured we call blessed. You have heard of the steadfastness of Job, and have seen what the Lord, who is compassionate and merciful, did in the end." (Divine Office page 132 James 5:7-11).

"Come and set us free, Lord God of power and might. Let your face shine upon us and we shall be saved. To Christ our Lord, who humbled himself for our sake, we joyfully say: Come, Lord Jesus!" (Divine Office page 133).

"Lord, make the peace we pray for a reality: may we live our days in quiet joy and, with the help of the Virgin Mary's prayers, safely reach your kingdom. Grant this through Christ our Lord. Let us praise the Lord. – And give him thanks." (Divine Office page 1026).

"Brothers, I do not want you to be ignorant of this mystery lest you be conceited. Just as you were once disobedient to God and now have received mercy through their disobedience, So the Jews have become disobedient-since God wished to show you mercy that they too may receive mercy. God had imprisoned all in disobedience that he might have mercy on all. How deep are the riches and the wisdom and the knowledge of God! How inscrutable His judgments, how unsearchable his ways! For "Who has known the mind of the Lord? Or who has been His counselor? Who has given Him anything so as to deserve return?" For from Him and through Him and for Him all things are. To Him is glory forever. Amen." (Divine Office page 705 Romans 11:25, 30-36).

"Father, the image of the Virgin is found in the Church. Mary had a faith that your Spirit prepared and a love that never knew sin, for you kept her sinless from the first moment of her conception. Trace in our actions the lines of her love, in our hearts her readiness of faith. Prepare once again a world for your Son who lives and reigns with you and the Holy Spirit, one God, forever and ever. May the Lord bless us, protect us from evil and bring us to everlasting life, Amen." (Little Office of the Blessed Virgin Mary: Page 42).

I AM PROCLAIMING THE GOOD NEWS AMONG THE NATIONS:

Because I started with Secret Sins: with Psalms 90:8 and then went to Ezekiel 33:10-20. I find it very important to share what we have done. We saw iniquity among us and people dieing because of it. So we the exiles traveled back to Babylon to make individual retribution for our sins, so that we would not die in our sins anymore: that we may live as the Lord lives. We have gotten right, just, and lawful with God our Father through Jesus Christ Crucified in the unity of the Holy Spirit. And we have done this while fasting: We in the spirit with and in Jesus have released the unbelievers and sinners from being bound unjustly. We all have also been justified by faith and by deeds done in Jesus Christ through the Holy Spirit in God's Almighty Power. We have shared our bread with the hungry, by offering them the body and blood of Jesus Christ. We have clothed the naked when we saw them, by giving then what was given to us. We have been washed clean by our Savior's precious blood. Jesus has wrapped us in His mantel of justice, and Jesus has robed us in His salvation and He has crowned us with His glory, like a bride bedecked with her jewels. I believe this exercise along with the exercise of God's Almighty Power and Jesus Christ Crucified through the Holy Spirit that we His children have received all we need to be enlightened. We don't have to dwell exiled from God, in death on a path to hell. Our free will has, is and always will be with us. Our cooperation and free will is the deciding factor in our lives as to where we dwell in this life and the life to come. Jesus Christ is offering the Way, Truth and Life to unbelievers and sinners, we can choose to love God and the things of God, and we can believe in His promises and His word. We can realize that heaven can be on earth inside of us individually through the Holy Spirit with and in Jesus Christ in God's Almighty Power. If we open our hearts and our lives to Jesus and Mary, the Trinity and Mary will come and make a home within each of us individually through the Holy Spirit in God's Almighty Power.

This battle against darkness within us can be won, individually with liberty and justice for all. "God did not send his Son into the world to condemn the world, but that the world might be saved through him." Convincing the world of sin means creating the conditions for its salvation. Awareness of our own sinfulness, including that which is inherited, is the first condition for salvation; the next is the confession of this sin before God, who desires only to receive this confession so that He can save man. To save means to embrace and lift up with redemptive love, with love that is always greater than any sin. In this regard the parable of the prodigal son is an unsurpassable paradigm." (Page 54 His Holiness John Paul ll Crossing The Threshold Of Hope.).

Salvation for Israel: "Good was to be hoped for, only from these who would pass through the purifying experience of the exile to form the New Israel." (Foot note from Jeremiah 24:1-10, Page 828 the Catholic Teen Bible NAB). The exiles will be the ones to form the New Israel. We have been given ample time between the fall of Jerusalem and the arrival of the fugitive from that city to journey to Babylon. We the survivors of the fall have returned to Babylon to make individual retribution for our sins. As we are fasting and traveling at the speed of light we the unbelievers and sinners are brought to Jerusalem, to the foot of the cross to die to sin and experience spiritual death with and in Jesus and Mary through the Holy Spirit in God's Almighty Power. That we also may live as the Lord lives. We have experienced death by the sword, which is the Word of God, as was Mary at the foot of the cross also. We have experienced regeneration of the Land. We have experienced regeneration of the People. Ezekiel has been released from dumbness, and the word of the Lord has came to Ezekiel saying "Thus I will display my glory among the nations, and all the nations shall see the judgment I have executed and the hand I have laid upon them. From that day forward the house of Israel shall know that I am the LORD, their God. The nations shall know that because of its sins the house of Israel went into exile; for they transgressed against me, and I hid my face from them and handed then over to their foes, so that all of them fell by the sword. According to their uncleanness and their transgressions I dealt with them, hiding my face from them.

Therefore, this says the Lord GOD: Now I will restore the fortunes of Jacob and have pity on the whole house of Israel, and I will be jealous for my holy name. They shall forget their disgrace and all the times they broke faith with me, when they live in security on their land with no one to frighten them. When I bring them back from among the peoples, I will gather them from the lands of their enemies, and will prove my holiness through them in the sight of many nations. Thus they shall know that I, the LORD, am their God, since I who exiled them among the nations, will gather them back on their land, not leaving any of them behind. No longer will I hide my face from them, for I have poured out my spirit upon the house of Israel, says the Lord God." (Ezekiel, 39:21-28 prove it! The Catholic Teen Bible NAB: Saint Jerome Press). From Secret Sins we the hearer's went back to Babylon to our spiritual captivity, we traveled at the speed of light and fasted so that the Word of God could recreate us the exiles, that were affected by the fall of Jerusalem and God's Word could continue to be faithful and true that no one has to be left 4 dead, or behind. That all unbelievers and sinners: could be brought to repentance and given the way the truth and life. We the living and the dead: could be gathered into the true Church of Jesus Christ. We the living and the dead:

would, and will become the New Israel. That we as a whole: then, now and in the future could behold all God's glory in the new heaven and new earth in the here and now, and forever more, Amen. Halleluiah, Halleluiah, Halleluiah. We are all loved and cherished children of God and He does not want any of His children to perish or suffer in their iniquity.

So in regard to fasting and traveling at the speed of light from Secret Sins: Isaiah 58:6-7 while fasting, the unbelievers and the sinners have and will be released from being bound unjustly, through faith and deeds done in Jesus Christ Crucified in God's Almighty Power through the Holy Spirit. We in the spirit have shared our bread with the hungry by offering them the body and blood of Jesus Christ. We have clothed the naked by giving them what was given to us. We have been washed clean by our Savior's precious blood and Jesus has wrapped us in His mantel of justice, we have all been robed in salvation, and have been crowned in His glory, like a bride bedecked with her jewels and this is only offered through Jesus Christ Crucified in God's Almighty Power through the Holy Spirit. We the bride's of Jesus Christ hope and pray this offering is pleasing to you dear sweet Father and that this brings a smile to your face and to your children in Jesus name Amen. Halleluiah!

"How Beautiful upon the mountains are the feet of him who brings glad tidings, Announcing peace, bearing good news, announcing salvation, and saying to Zion, "Your God is King!" Hark! Your watchmen raise a cry, together they shout for joy, for they see directly, before their eyes, the Lord restoring Zion. Break out together in song, O ruins of Jerusalem! For the Lord comforts his people, he redeems Jerusalem. The Lord has bared his holy arm in the sight of all the nations; all the ends of the earth will behold the salvation of our God." (Divine Office page 212 Isaiah 52:7-10).

"Send the fire of your Holy Spirit deep within us, Lord, so that we can serve you with chaste bodies and please you with pure minds. I put all my trust in you Lord." (Divine Office page 1018).

"Almighty God, ever-living mystery of unity and trinity, you gave life to the new Israel by birth from water and the Spirit, and made it a chosen race, a royal priesthood, a people set apart as your eternal possession. May all those you have called to walk in the splendor of the new light render you fitting service and adoration. All power is yours, Lord God, our mighty King, alleluia." (Divine Office page 714).

"Give us grace to see thee, Lord. Mirrored in Thy Holy Word may we imitate you now, and be pure, as pure art thou, that we like to thee may be at thy great Epiphany, and may praise thee, ever Blessed, God in man made manifest. All praise to God the Father who brought His chosen people to rebirth from imperishable seed through His eternal Word." (   )

THE CATHOLIC TEEN BIBLE NAB SAINT JEROME PRESS DOGMATIC CONSTITUTION ON DIVINE REVELAION:

1. Preface
2. Revelation itself
7. Handing on Divine Revelation
11. Sacred Scripture, Its Inspiration and divine interpretation
14. The Old Testament
17. The New Testament- the Mystery had not been manifested to other generations as it was now revealed to His Apostles and Prophets in the Holy Spirit, so that they might preach the gospel, stir up faith in Jesus, Christ and Lord and gather together the Church
21. Sacred Scripture In The Life Of The Church.

To "Summa it up" Thomas Aquinas would say. You realize through your tribulations in your life all that ISRAEL is: through Him, with Him, in Him in the Unity of the Holy Spirit all Glory and Honor is Yours Almighty Father, forever and ever, Amen. Only through Almighty Power and Jesus Christ Crucified through the Holy Spirit.

THE NARROW GATE IS THE WORD OF GOD MANIFESTED IN US:

"Lord, who at your first Eucharist did pray that all your Church might be for ever one, Grant us at every Eucharist to say with longing heart and soul, "Your will be done." O may we all one bread, one body be, Through this blest Sacrament of Unity.

For all your Church, O Lord, we intercede; O make our lack of charity to cease; Draw us the nearer each to each, we plead, By drawing all to you, O Prince of Peace; Thus may we all one bread, one body be, Through this blest Sacrament of Unity.

We pray then, too, for wand'rers from your fold; O bring them back, good Shepherd of the sheep, Back to the faith which saints believed of old, Back to the Church which still that faith does keep; Soon may we all one bread, one body be, Through this blest Sacrament of Unity.

So, Lord, at length when sacraments shall cease, May we be one with all your Church above, One with your saints in one unending peace, One with your saints in one unbounded love; More blessed still in peace and love to be One with the Trinity in Unity. (Divine Office Melody 134 page 1565).

DAWN OF THE AGES

"What joy, what happiness there is in Heaven! The shoot from the root of Jesse, sown so long ago in the time of the patriarchs, has today sprung up and begun to grow, and will bear a Flower which is destined to heal the world, a Flower whose scent revives the dead, whose taste heals the sick, and whose beauty delights the angels – a white and red Flower which angels long to see.

As Bernard says: "Rejoice, father Adam, but even more you, mother Eve, exult, who as you were the parents of all were also the destroyers of all, and what is worse, destroyers before you were parents.

So both of you must take comfort from your daughter, and such a daughter too. What was it, Adam, you said? It was the women who gave me fruit from the tree, and so I ate it. Now today a woman is returned to you for a woman, a prudent woman for a foolish one, a humble for a proud, one who is to offer you the taste of life instead of the tree of death, and produce the sweetness of eternal fruit instead of the bitterness of that poisonous food.

A virgin to be admired and most worthy of every honor! A woman to be uniquely revered, wonderful above all women, the savior of her parents and giver of life to her descendants."

Let us then throw ourselves at the feet of this holy Sibyl, and pour out our prayers with exultant spirit and sing praises while our hearts dance with joy: let us place ourselves under her protection, and cry aloud: Therefore, you our Advocate, Our Lady, our delight, therefore turn your merciful eyes toward us, and after our exile show us Jesus, the blessed fruit of your womb.

It is him we seek, him we gasp for, hastening toward him, desiring him with all the ardor of our hearts. It is you, Virgin, who must direct us, you must lead us to him, lead us to where he reigns, and show him to us, crowned with glory and honor, surrounded by angels, seated on the highest throne at the right hand of the Father, reigning with him, and governing the whole world together with him.

For a long time I have wondered and been at a loss to understand why the evangelists should have spoken at such length about John the Baptist and the other apostles, and yet told us so little about the Virgin Mary, who in life and distinction excels them all. Being at a loss, as I say, to understand this, all I can think is that it pleased the Holy Spirit that it should be so.

It was by the providence of the Holy Spirit that the evangelists kept silent, because the glory of the Virgin, as we read in the psalms, was all within, and could more truly be thought of than described. The outline of her life: that Jesus was born of her is enough to tell her whole story. What more do you seek for in the Virgin? It is enough for you that she is the Mother of God. What beauty, I ask you, what virtue, what perfection, what grace, what glory does not belong to the Mother of God?

The Holy Spirit has not described her in words, but has left her to you to picture in your own mind, so that you may understand that there was nothing she lacked of grace, perfection, or glory which could be imagined in the mind of a chaste human being, or rather that in fact she surpassed all understanding. So when she was wholly perfect, it would not have been right to describe her in part, for fear that you might think she would have lacked what had not been described. To say of the Virgin Mary only that she is the Mother of God surpasses all that can be said under God.

What a marvelous woman, to be the mother of her own Creator! What an amazing distinction for a woman, to have a Son in common with God. The Father loves his Son; the Mother rejoices in her Son. The Father tells his Son: From the womb, before the morning star, I begot you; the Mother says to her same Son: From the womb, I, a virgin, brought you into the world. She is amazed at her own glory, nor can she herself understand her elevation, for by the very fact of being made mother of the Creator she became with the best right mistress and queen of all creation. Truly, Mary, he who is powerful did great things for you; truly because he made you his own mother, all the generations of the ages will call you blessed." (Little Office of the Blessed Virgin Mary pages 180,181,182,183 from a sermon by Saint Thomas of Villanova, bishop).

CREATION

In the Holy Spirit through Jesus Christ Crucified we the living can die to sin and experience spiritual death with our Mother Mary alongside Jesus Christ' death through God's Almighty Power and we can be resurrected spiritually and physically and given everlasting life in the new heaven and new earth or reject His grace and condemn themselves and suffer. In Jesus Christ Crucified with God's Almighty Power the dead can be resurrected from their sleep and given everlasting life in heaven. Or to eternal damnation, depending on each person's freewill. We the living and the dead can live spiritual lives in the new heaven and new earth now and forever more through the Holy Spirit. In the Unity of the Holy Spirit all Glory and Honor is yours Almighty Father forever and ever. We have done this, while we have time, and we celebrate this Amazing Privilege with equality for all.

It's not what we look like, or what we wear, it's what's in our heart that makes us beautiful and enables our mind to conceive the Holy Spirit and give birth to Jesus Christ in us. So you see we will not all at the same time give birth to the child Jesus in us. This is why it says we must be a child to enter into the kingdom of God.

SPIRITUAL CREATION:

We the living and the dead can die to sin and experience spiritual death and or physical death with and in Jesus in Mind, Body, Soul, and Spirit in God's Almighty Power through the Holy Spirit in this life, and or the life to come only through Him, with Him, in Him, in the Unity of the Holy Spirit can we be resurrected from the grave and be born again and or reborn and given a new spiritual life with and in Jesus Christ through the Holy Spirit in God's Almighty Power, that we may dwell with and in Him in the new heaven and new earth. The living and the dead that are living spiritually in Jesus Christ' body can be resurrected from their sleep and be born again and or reborn unto everlasting life in heaven on earth.

We the living can say "yes, come Lord Jesus," We can be washed with the water of baptism, thus washes away our sin. We can be made in God's image and the child Jesus can be conceived by us individually without sin through the Holy Spirit; we can experience an immaculate conception. We can give birth to Jesus Christ in us, in the Unity of the Holy Spirit and in God's Almighty Power; we can offer up to God, Jesus' great sacrifice when our world ends by the baptism of fire, death unto everlasting life in the new heaven and new earth through the Holy Spirit.

We the living and the dead can be given truth, we can believe that the old world has passed away to the spirit and we have become the New Israel. All of us one with and in Christ, the members of His Body, The Bride, The Church, The City of God can dwell within us, in the here and now, and forever more.

And we can live in peace with God, Jesus, and Mary our Mother, Joseph her husband and all the angels, Martyrs and saints that have done our Father's Will. Including all the people that we love that have gone to heaven that live on earth with us, we can be with them, we can see them and they can see us and we can enjoy each other.

And we as a whole as the members of Jesus' Holy and Sacred Body can celebrate this Paschal Mystery of our Death and our Resurrection, our Ascension into heaven with and in Jesus every time the Priest and the Church which is us come together for this service during Mass. Then all Honor, Glory and Power is given to Almighty Father through the Holy Spirit with and in Jesus Christ Crucified. We are commanded to serve and to be servants of the Lord and to serve God through our brothers and sisters The Catholic Church offers this service at Mass, on a daily basis to all God's children forever and ever. Amen.

I am handing to your Head Good Works for the Treasury. I love you as Christ loves me, and as God loves Christ, The Bride. We can enter into the Glory of God and His Kingdom. The Mystery of the Church of God through the Holy Spirit has been revealed through Jesus Christ' Bride through God's Almighty Power. This beautiful kingdom of God is to be revered, and to be held high. That the love and respect that we hold in our hearts for the Trinity: might always be displayed in our Fathers Universal word throughout the Universe. At this very moment our hearts should be melting into pure gold and the street of the city pure gold also, transparent as glass. "Let us rejoice and exult and give him the glory, for the marriage of the Lamb has come, and his bride has made herself ready; to her it has been granted to be clothed with fine linen, bright and pure" – for the fine linen is the righteous deeds of the saints." (Revelations 19:7-9). I have not written this scroll to replace the Bible, but to edify, with moral and spiritual love, that we as a whole, all denominations would grow and become more perfect in Jesus Christ' body. My prayers are that this exercise would purify our mind, body, soul and spirit and that we would be lead of our own free will to embrace the Holy Bible that we would have a better understanding of what it is saying, that we all might be found, and that iniquity would cease, that we as a whole would live as the Lord lives. I am requesting a privilege from the Catholic Church to share my revelations of Revelation itself. I offer all through Jesus Christ Crucified, in God's Almighty Power through the Holy Spirit with and in my Loving Daughter, Sister and our Ever Virgin Mother Mary's Hands.

"God's Saving Action as summed up in the Isaiah story continues to be repeated throughout our lives. We are constantly being delivered from death to life if we are willing to cooperate. Change, especially when it is thrust upon us rather than chosen, is rarely, welcomed. We can feel anxious and even angry and resist the very things that will eventually prove to be life-giving. Worst of all, we so desperately want to hold on to the way things used to be that we entirely miss the gifts to be found in the present moment." (Spurgeons).

Heavenly Father, give us eyes to see the wonder, and the truth of your faithfulness. I hope and pray that this message of revelation itself will reach the Pope and all God's children, that we can receive it as food and share it with all God's Children, enabling them to all have Bright Futures.

"Let Israel rejoice in you, Lord, and acknowledge you as creator and redeemer, we put our trust in your faithfulness and proclaim the Wonderful Truths of Salvation.

May your Loving Kindness embrace us now and forever." (Divine Office pages: 710, and 711).

"May your Holy Spirit teach us to do your Will today, and may your Wisdom guide us always. Each Sunday give us the joy of gathering around your table of your Word and Your Body: From our hearts we thank you- for countless Blessings." (Divine Office pages: 711, and 712).

LORD, INCREASE OUR FAITH!

"The apostles said to the Lord, "Increase our faith!" The Lord replied, "If you had faith the size of a mustard seed, you could say to this mulberry tree, 'Be uprooted and planted in the sea,' and it would obey you.

"Who among you would say to your slave who has just come in from plowing or tending sheep in the field, 'Come here at once and take your place at the table'?

Would you not rather say to him, 'Prepare supper for me, put on your apron and serve me while I eat and drink; later you may eat and drink'?

Do you thank the slave for doing what was commanded? So you also, when you have done all that you were ordered to do, say, 'We are worthless slaves; we have done only what we ought to have done!' " (Luke 17 5-19).

BEING MINDFUL OF GOD... MAKES ROOM FOR GODS WORD

"Prepare a path in our hearts for the coming of your word, - and let his glory be revealed among us. Bring low the mountains of our pride, - and fill up the valleys of our weakness. Break down the wall of hatred that divides the nations, - and make level for mankind the paths to peace." (Divine Office page 52).

"HAIL, MARY... BEHOLD, YOU WILL CONCEIVE IN YOUR WOMB AND BEAR A SON, AND YOU SHALL NAME HIM JESUS." (Luke 1:31).

"While Mary contemplated all she had come to know through reading, listening and observing, she grew in faith, increased in merits, and was more illuminated by wisdom and more consumed by the fire of charity. The heavenly mysteries were opened to her, and she was filled with joy; she became fruitful by the Spirit, was being directed toward God, and watched over protectively while on earth.

So remarkable are the divine graces that they elevate one from the lowest depths to the highest summit, and transform one to a greater holiness. How entirely blessed was the mind of the Virgin which, through the indwelling and guidance of the Spirit, was always and in every way open to the power of the Word of God. She was not led by her own senses, nor by her own will; thus she accomplished outwardly through her body what wisdom from within gave to her faith.

It was fitting for divine Wisdom, which created itself a home in the Church, to use the intervention of the most blessed Mary in guarding the law, purifying the mind, giving an example of humility and providing a spiritual sacrifice.

Imitate her, O faithful soul. Enter into the deep recesses of your heart so that you may be purified spiritually and cleansed from your sins. God places more value on good will in all we do than on the works themselves.

Therefore, whether we give ourselves to God in the work of contemplation or whether we serve the needs of our neighbor by good works, we accomplish these things because the love of Christ urges us on. The acceptable offering of the spiritual purification is accomplished not in a man-made temple but in the recesses of the heart where the Lord Jesus freely enters." (From a sermon by Saint Lawrence Justinian, bishop (Sermo 8, in festo Purifcationis B.V.M.: Opera, 2 Venetiis 1751, 38-39. Little Office of the Blessed Virgin Mary Page 113, 114).

Mary is a beacon to the will of God for us. She gave birth literally and in the Spirit. In our Spirituality we are to do the same without sin. "Our King and our God, you have raised us up by your coming, help us to honor you all the days of our lives by our faith and our deeds." (Little Office of the Blessed Virgin Mary, Page 22). The glory of the Lord is anything bringing worship, adoration, praise. The condition of the highest achievement, splendor, prosperity. The highest decree of pleasure, satisfaction, pride; magnificence, radiance. Tiss heaven or the bliss of heaven. Glorying – to be very proud, rejoice. Exult. Have you been glorified in the Lord? If so celebrate with festive celebration.

"You were dead through the trespasses and sins in which you once lived, following the course of this world, following the ruler of the power of the air, the spirit that is now at work among those who are disobedient.

All of us once lived among them in the passions of our flesh, following the desires of flesh and senses, and we were by nature children of wrath, like everyone else.

But God, who is rich in mercy, out of the great love with which he loved us even when we were dead through our trespasses, made us alive together with Christ – by grace you have been saved – and raised us up with him and seated us with him in the heavenly places in Christ Jesus, so that in the ages to come he might show the immeasurable riches of his grace in kindness toward us in Christ Jesus.

For by grace you have been saved through faith, and this is not your own doing; it is the gift of God – not the result of works, so that no one may boast. For we are what he has made us, created in Christ Jesus for good works, which God prepared beforehand to be our way of life." (Ephesians 2: 1-10)

He would see for Himself whether all men had forsaken Him. We have Free Will. Do not forsake Him. You also will feel forsaken through your tribulations and trails, but we know we must mirror our Lord in all things. "He was heard because of His reverence." (Hebrews 5:7).

"Blessed be God, the giver of salvation, who decreed that mankind should become a new creation in himself when all would be made new. With great confidence let us ask him: Lord, renew us in your Spirit. Lord, you promised a new heaven and a new earth renew us daily through your Spirit, that we may enjoy your Presence for ever in the heavenly Jerusalem.

Help us to work with you to make this world alive with your Spirit, and to build on earth a city of justice, love and peace. Free us from all negligence and sloth, and give us joy in your gifts of grace. Deliver us from evil, and from slavery to the senses, which blinds us to goodness." (Divine Office page 279).

PRAY THE OUR FATHER

Our Father who art in heaven, hollowed be thy name, thy kingdom come thy will be done on earth as it is in heaven. Give us this day our daily bread and forgive us our trespasses as we forgive those who trespass against us and lead us not into temptation but deliver us from evil, Amen.

"Now, from the heav'ns descending, is seen a glorious light, The Bride of Christ in splendor, Arrayed in purest white. She is the holy City, Whose radiance is the grace Of all the saints in glory, From every time and place.

This is the hour of gladness for Bridegroom and for Bride, The Lamb's great feast is ready, His Bride is at his side. How bless'd are these invited to share his wedding feast: The least become the greatest, The greatest are the least.

He who is throned in Heaven takes up his dwelling place Among his chosen people, Who see him face to face. No sound is heard of weeping, For pain and sorrow cease, And sin shall reign no longer, But love and joy and peace.

See how a new creation is brought at last to birth, A new and glorious heaven, a new and glorious earth. Death's power for ever broken, its empire swept away, The promised dawn of glory Begins its endless day." (Divine Office page 1585 Hymn 178).

"Draw us beyond the limits which this world imposes, to the life where your spirit makes all life complete we ask this through Christ our Lord." (Divine Office page 217).

"Be kind to one another, compassionate, and mutually forgiving, just as God has forgiven you in Christ. Be imitators of God as his dear children. Follow the way of love, even as Christ loved you. He gave Himself for us as an offering to God, a gift of pleasing fragrance." (Divine Office page 376 Ephesians 4:32 – 5:2).

"Gather into your Church those who do not yet believe, and help them to build it up by good deeds done for love of thee." (Divine Office pages 376 and 377).

"We see Jesus crowned with glory and honor because he suffered death, that through God's gracious will he might taste death for the sake of all men. Indeed, it was fitting that when bringing many sons to glory God, for whom and through whom all things exist, should make their leader in the work of salvation perfect through suffering." (Divine Office page 377 Hebrews 2:0-10).

LOVE IS NOTHING, BUT EVERYTHINK!

This is the War of Armageddon that happens through Him, with Him, in Him in the Unity of the Holy Spirit, all Glory and Honor are yours Almighty Father, forever and ever, Amen. We can unite with Jesus Christ. It's a Spiritual Battle: Our Lord and Savior Jesus Christ has already defeated the beast and the devil. Our Lord is seated at the right hand of God reigning in heaven, until the end of time. In the end when our Lord comes into our hearts and our lives our battle is not against flesh and blood, but against principalities, powers, and the forces of darkness. God sent His Son, His only begotten in the likeness of Him, to suffer and to die for the sins of the world, that we His children could come to the truth, and live spiritual lives through the body and blood of our Savior Jesus Christ with and in the Trinity through the Holy Spirit of God. And this gift is offered through Jesus Christ Crucified. When we learn how important spiritual life is, it becomes the most glorious day of our lives. God the Father offers unending life in heaven on earth through the Holy Spirit into our lives with and in His Son to all that would accept and believe now and after physical death. If we wait for physical death to experience spiritual life, you could say that we died in sin at physical dead. Thank God, Jesus is their waiting at the gates of hell, offering a better way.

WHY DO CATHOLICS DO THAT?

I would like to share with all my brothers and sisters our spiritual life that we can experience through our sacraments that can lead all people, from the coming of Jesus Christ to life in the New Heaven and New Earth.

We find all glory and honor serving our Father in heaven and on earth. Our mind, body, soul and spirit can be caught on fire and we can be filled with love for the Prophets and the Saints and those men and women who are friends of Christ's. It's really nice having all the right friends in all the right places. Alleluia.

1. Baptism + Yes, Come Lord Jesus. We are made in God's image.
2. Confirmation + We Conceive the Holy Spirit without sin.
3. Eucharist + Conception. The Lord is being formed in us.
4. Penance + Birth. We give birth to Jesus in us spiritually.
5. Holy Orders + Death. We die to sin and experience spiritual death and or physical death with and in our Lord Jesus Christ Crucified in God's Almighty Power.
6. Matrimony + Life. Resurrected from spiritual death and or physical death with and in Jesus Christ Crucified in God's Almighty Power.
7. Extreme Unction + Heaven. We the living and the dead ascend to the Throne with and in Jesus Christ to dwell with and in Him in the new heaven and new earth, spiritually, and physically. This is the New Israel, the land of Promise.

In our spirituality I have explained our spiritual life with and in the Lord. They are stages 1-7, given to your head on 8-09-2010, it is all there. There will not be another day like this for a thousand years. Pray brothers and sisters that you could walk with God. Enoch walked with God without dieing.

"The whole Church is a priestly people. Through Baptism all the faithful share in the priesthood of Christ. This participation is called the "common priesthood of the faithful." Based on this common priesthood and ordered to its service, there exists another participation in the mission of Christ: the ministry conferred by the sacrament of Holy Orders, where the task is to serve in the name and in the person of Christ the Head in the midst of the community." (CCC. #1590). "With the Lord there is mercy and fullness of
Redemption, Israel He will redeem from all its iniquity." (Psalm: 130).

"Praise the Lord for he is good; sing to our God for he is loving: to him our praise is due. The Lord builds up Jerusalem and brings back Israel's exiles, he heals the broken-hearted, and He binds up all their wounds. He fixes the number of the stars; he calls each one by its name. Our Lord is great and almighty; his wisdom can never be measured. The Lord raises the lowly; he humbles the wicked to the dust. O sing to the Lord, giving thanks; sing psalms to our God with the harp. He covers the heavens with clouds; he prepares the rain for the earth, making mountains sprout with grass* and with plants to serve man's needs. He provides the beasts with their food and young ravens that call upon him. His delight is not in horses nor his pleasure in warriors' strength. The Lord delights in those who revere him, in those who wait for his love." (Psalm 147:1-11).

The greatest wonder of all is: Gods amazing love for mankind in sending His only Son Jesus to set us free and give us everlasting life. The splendor of a king clothed in majesty let all the earth rejoice, all the earth rejoice. He wraps Himself in light, in darkness trys to hide it trembles at His voice, trembles at His voice. How great is our God, Sing with me how great is our God. And all will see how great, how great is our God, sing with me how great is our God, and all will see how great, how great is our God.

Chapter 3

March 25, 2010 Feast of the Annunciation

On March 23, 2010, Two days before the Annunciation the spirit moved me to start writing, so all day I wrote pertaining to my vision and dream and of secret sins. The next day I put it all together and typed. On the morning of March 25th I printed it. I emailed it to everyone on my list. Also, I handed it out at church. I am very excited to share my experience with you.

When I was writing about God's Word being alive, it truly became alive. At one moment all the words on my sheet of paper jumped off the paper and started dancing and moving around on my table for a few seconds. It was quite delightful to watch my Lord speak to me in this way. I was not in mediation to invoke this. I had never seen anything like this before. Then all of a sudden they were all back on my paper where they were supposed to be. I also sent a copy to the Pope and to the Bishop's "Assistant Chancellor" in Phoenix Arizona. I had wanted to write everything down for years, but I just did not know how to put on paper what was in my heart and in my life.

Getting back to the Feast of the Annunciation, which we as Catholics celebrate on March 25th. The Annunciation means we are commemorating the announcement of the Incarnation by the angel Gabriel to the Virgin Mary. There are references to the feast as early as the fifth century. Its date was finally determined by the date of Christmas on December 25. It is a feast of the Blessed Virgin. I truly believe that it is God's will for His children to follow our Mother Mary and say "yes, come Lord Jesus," and to conceive as she did. Our conception is spiritual.

"Here is a Hymn I love it goes like this, Mary was first and foremost in fullness of grace and she embodies all that God taught our race. It goes like this. "O Mary, of all women thou art the chosen one, who ancient prophets promised would bear

God's only Son; all Hebrew generations prepared the way to thee, that in your womb the God-man might come to set man free. O Mary you embody all God taught to our race, for you are first and foremost in fullness of His grace; we praise this wondrous honor that you gave birth to Him who from you took His manhood and saved us from our sin." (Little Office of the Blessed Virgin Mary: page 70).

When Christ comes He baptizes us with fire through the Holy Spirit and with God's Almighty Power. We should prepare our mind, body soul and spirit to allow the Holy Spirit and Jesus Christ to recreate us. This fire is a key element in His love. It can set our whole body on fire; our body is made of the earth and God's spirit. And this fire and His Spirit tells us there is a better way to live. He tells us that He loves us and that He has given us free will. We can accept His free gift of love and grace and experience His Almighty Power and His Divine Mercy, through trusting in Him and in everything He has told us. At that moment we are lead to Christ Crucified and we realize that there is nothing that He will not forgive. We truly have to believe, trust and have faith in Him and surrender and submit to God, so that He can heal us. If you are taken in the spirit to the day and time of Jesus Christ Crucifixion you will also see Jesus Christ's Mother there with Him! This is the location that the Holy Man in the Temple, Simeon prophesied about her heart that it would be pierced with a sword. This happened to Mary when they pierced Jesus' side with a lance. Oh, what pain and suffering they endured at Calvary. Brothers and Sisters do not be deceived. Mary from the first moment of her conception was born without sin, yet she experienced spiritual death with and in Jesus Christ, in God's Almighty Power. And She did spiritually die for the sins of the world with Jesus Christ at His Crucifixion. And this is where we find the word co-redemptrix. When Jesus was resurrected from the dead and when He ascended to His Throne, Mary was also spiritually taken. And then at her death she ascended body and soul to heaven to spend eternity with Her Son in the Kingdom of God. "Co-Redemptrix means a title of the Blessed Virgin as co-operator with Christ in the work of human redemption. It may be considered an aspect of Mary's mediation in not only consenting to become the Mother of God but in freely consenting in his labors, sufferings, and death for the salvation of the human race. As Co-Redemptrix, she is in no sense equal to Christ in his redemptive activity, since she herself required redemption and in fact was redeemed by her Son. He alone merited man's salvation. Mary effectively interceded to obtain subjective application of Christ's merits to those whom the Savior had objectively redeemed." (Modern Catholic Dictionary John A. Hardon, S.J.). So in our spiritual existence we also are under Mary's shadow and spiritually we are also Co-Remptrix like Mary. We the living need to concentrate in the here and now and realize that everything Mary has done we are to do also spiritually and physically, if we want to become Perfect as our Father commands us to do, and likewise we are to follow Jesus Christ God's Son from the Annunciation to Pentecost and with and in His Glorious Ascension into heaven, in the here and now, and for all eternity.

Christ comes with bright light into the darkness within us and can set us free. The beast that is in control of the world that is in us no longer has to rule; rather we can ask Jesus Christ into our heart and our lives. And all of this happens in the twinkling of an eye. We the living can unite in the spirit at Jesus Christ' death and we can be resurrected from our grave and we can experience spiritual death with Jesus and Mary and be given spiritual life with and in Jesus and Mary in the new heaven and new earth in the here and now, before we physically die. We can realize we are immortal beings and we can become more like Jesus and Mary a spiritual being, we can ask God through Jesus Christ to please heal us, and with our cooperation we can be given an immaculate mind, body, soul and spirit, spiritually and physically through the Holy Spirit. The definition of immaculate is perfectly clean, without a spot or stain, unsoiled, perfectly correct, without a flaw, fault, or error, pure, innocent, without sin. The New Israel is the new people of God in the splendor of the Trinity. Because of our spiritual death, we live unto the Lord in Jesus Christ Body, and Jesus' Body is very Holy and Pure, this is what we of the spirit are made of, the most beautiful body ever created.

Our Mother Mary is beside us at our moment of spiritual death. The moment we die to sin, is also when our spiritual death takes place at Jesus' crucifixion. And so in this way some of Mary's promises are obtainable now also. For example, Mary also said she would be with us at our moment of death, and she was and is and will be for all eternity. The word world is symbolic of each of us, and the things that are going on inside of us are described as what is taking place in the world. So when we unite with Jesus Christ Crucified in mind, body, soul and spirit we have obtained world peace. We have been reconciled to God with and in Jesus Christ Crucified through the Holy Spirit. Jesus Christ has made Atonement for us by His perfect act of love. When we unite with Jesus Christ we are reconciled to our Father. Reconciled means we are no longer separated from God and the things of God, there is no more warring within us due to sin. This is what our Mother Mary spoke of in her apparitions. Mary spoke of this at Fatima, in 1917. Mary said her immaculate heart would triumph and it would bring in an era of peace. No more warring we are at peace with God and all this happened within us, the world. Our mind body soul and spirit are at peace. Mary the mother of Jesus asked us to seek God while we have time and to repent, to convert, pray and fast so that at the coming of her Son we would be prepared. When we allow Jesus into our hearts and our lives we can also let the spirit and Fire consume us totally.

We have, are, and will become Holy in different ways, we are all one through the Holy spirit of Jesus Christ. We are one though many in the body of Jesus Christ and we all have been given different functions pertaining to Christ' body. I really enjoy watching people, especially those that love God and the things of God, some of us are really busy, helping in many different ways, some of us need help from others, we all work together to make the body the best it can be. And I am very grateful for the unity we share in His body. I am grateful for the sanctifying grace that God has given us, it produces in us holiness through the exercise of God's Almighty Power with and in Jesus Christ Crucified that we may participate in divine life. "Holiness, Essential. Also called substantial holiness, is the possession of sanctifying grace. It is present in a person from the moment of baptism and represents that person's likeness to God. As such it is independent of the person's moral conduct. It is intrinsic goodness or goodness of being and is the basic reason why the New Testament speaks of the faithful as 'saints.' They are holy insofar as they are pleasing to God." (Modern Catholic Dictionary John A. Hardon, S. J.). "He has blessed us in the Beloved." (Ephesians 1:6). This Blessed Holiness can lead us to another promise. (At this very moment there is thunder and lightening bolts all around me.) We would be able to see the new heaven and new earth come down from heaven from our Father in the land of the living.

So only in a spiritual and physical way does the world end. Spiritually and physically are we changed. In the Book of Revelations when John was describing the destruction of the world it was a symbolic description of our spiritual death mind body soul and spirit. We the living can become what we were created for, to serve God in Holiness and to do His will rejoicing, that Jesus has brought us into His light, world without end. Amen. Amen. Yes, Come Lord Jesus, We can conceive the Holy Spirit without sin in our mind body soul and spirit. We can have a conception in our bodies, and we can give spiritual birth to the word of God. Our mind body soul and spirit can spiritually die to sin with and in Christ at His crucifixion. God can raise us from our grave and we can be resurrected from our spiritual death through the Holy Spirit to spiritual life with and in Jesus Christ, through God's Almighty Power. We can find ourselves with and in the new heaven and new earth with Jesus Christ and the Holy Ones of God knowing we shall never die.

"End of the World. Revealed truth that the present world of space and time will come to an end. It will be on the day when the dead will rise from the grave and Christ will appear in his majesty to judge the human race. As to the manner of the world's destruction or its time, nothing definite can be said whether from natural science or from the Christian faith. The idea of destruction by fire (11 Peter 3:7, 10, 12) can be taken simply as a current mode of expression to state that the present world will be dissolved and a new world will come into existence". (Modern Catholic Dictionary John A. Hardon, S. J.). "Thus says the Lord God: O my people, I will open your graves and have you rise from them, and bring you back to the land of Israel. Then you shall know that I am the Lord, when I open your graves and have you rise from them, O my people! I will put my spirit in you that you may live, and I will settle you upon your land, thus you shall know that I am the Lord. I have promised, and I will do it, says the Lord." (Ezekiel 37: 23b-14). So in this way: Oneness of spirit, praising and glorifying our Father in Heaven, all His children in proper order, thank you Father Time for loving us with everlasting Truth. We have obtained supernatural merit; we have received an increase of sanctifying grace, eternal life. We have died to sin, in our Lord's divine friendship. We have been raised from our graves in God's Almighty Power. Thus an increase of heavenly glory. We thank you Father, Son and Holy Spirit for our spiritual gifts, our Mother Mary and all your children.

"Blessed Lady, sky and stars, earth and rivers, day and night – everything that is subject to the power or use of man – rejoice that through you they are in some sense restored to their lost beauty and are endowed with inexpressible new grace. All creatures were dead, as it were, useless for human beings or for the praise of God, who made them.

The world, contrary to its true destiny, was corrupted and tainted by the acts of human beings who served idols. Now all creation has been restored to life and rejoices that it is controlled and given splendor by those who believe in God.

The universe rejoices with new and indefinable loveliness. Not only does it feel the unseen presence of God himself, its Creator, it sees him openly, working and making it holy. These great blessings spring from the blessed fruit of Mary's womb.

Through the fullness of the grace that was given you, dead things rejoice in their freedom, and those in heaven are glad to be made new. Through the Son who was the glorious fruit of your virgin womb, just souls who died before his life-giving death rejoice as they are freed from captivity and the angels are glad at the restoration of their shattered domain.

Lady, full and overflowing with grace, all creation received new life from your abundance. Virgin, blessed above all creatures, through your blessing all creation is blessed, not only creation from its Creator, but the Creator himself has been blessed by creation.

To Mary God gave his only-begotten Son, whom he loved as himself. Through Mary God made himself a Son, not different but the same, by nature Son of God and Son of Mary.

The whole universe was created by God, and God was born of Mary. God created all things, and Mary gave birth to God. The God who made all things gave himself form through Mary, and thus he made his own creation. He who could create all things from nothing would not remake his ruined creation without Mary.

God, then, is the Father of the created world and Mary the mother of the re-created world. God is the Father by whom all things were given life, and Mary the mother through whom all things were given new life.

For God begot the Son, through whom all things were made, and Mary gave birth to him as the Savior of the world. Without God's Son, nothing could exist, without Mary's Son, nothing could be redeemed.

Truly the Lord is with you, to whom the Lord granted that all nature should owe as much to you as to himself." (Little Office of the Blessed Virgin Mary pages 38, 39 and 40 from a sermon by Saint Anselm, bishop).

"God is King" He rules the world with justice, and He judges people with truth, praise to you dear sweet Father, Son and Holy Spirit, Most blessed Trinity.

I have learned that when we are sick and tired of being sick and tired of doing our own will and have dug a hole so deep that its almost impossible to get out of, that's when the stubborn will turn to God and will ask for help.

And we can realize that where Christ is Mary is also. We can become very humble and seek the will of God. We know we are forgiven because of His Divine Mercy.

After Mary's beautiful Immaculate Heart has triumphed, we His children seek only to please our Father and Mother in Heaven.

So we take great pleasure in doing His will, the fruit that comes is truly divine. Nothing compares to His goodness.

In this way the fruit of evil has been destroyed and has made room for the fruit of God. We can be consumed by God and can be drawn by Jesus Christ to our consummation. Brothers and Sisters this chastisement we go through is absolutely vital. It can create in us virtues we never thought possible. "Only when we allow Jesus Christ in our hearts and our lives are we to receive the full measure of His love." (Mary Burrill).

The Sacraments are a mystery, we are being consecrated through them and they are sacred. In Christianity any of certain rites ordained by Jesus, (It is our Pledge). This pledge is the way the truth and life. "Through these Sacraments and in our spiritual life we are able to receive unique precious personal graces" (Father Larry Baumann): 1. Baptism + Yes, Come Lord Jesus. And we are made in God's image. 2. Confirmation + We conceive the Holy Spirit without sin. 3. Eucharist + Conception. The Lord is being formed in us. 4. Penance + Birth. We give birth to Jesus in us spiritually. 5. Holy Orders + Death. We die to sin and experience spiritual death or physical death with and in our Lord Jesus Christ Crucified in God's Almighty Power. 6. Matrimony + Life. Resurrected from spiritual death or physical death with and in Jesus Christ Crucified in God's Almighty Power. 7. Extreme Unction + Heaven. We the living and the dead ascend to the throne with and in Jesus Christ to dwell with and in Him in the new heaven and new earth, spiritually and physically. This is the New Israel, the land of Promise.

At Pentecost when the Spirit descended with fire on the Apostles and disciples, they were enlightened as you can be. You can become disciples also. And this can happen all around the world and it can be spoken in all languages through His disciples. We can live with and in the Word of God and we can bring the peace of God to our brothers and sisters teaching all nations.

With Mary at the annunciation we can say 'yes' come Lord Jesus, and with God's Almighty Power and Christ Crucified we can conceive the Holy Spirit without sin. The Lord stirs in us like He did Mary and we have a conception like our Mother Mary. We give birth to Jesus, Mary's son. We can die to sin and experience spiritual death with God's Almighty Power with and in Jesus Christ Crucified and with Mary Jesus' Mother, and our Mother also. We can be reborn and or resurrected and we can ascend to the Throne in one spirit and one body with and in Jesus Christ and we can live with all the Holy Ones that have done Gods will in the new heaven and new earth.

At this monumental moment we find ourselves making sweet love with Almighty God, our faithful and true friend by being obedient to His Word, We are His Brides.

So in this "Way" we are not committing adultery, we are not being idol, and we can be faithful to our Maker, our Lord and Master our loving Husband. Jesus brings fire and the spirit at Pentecost, then and now and forever more.

This fire is all consuming and "re-creates" us like our Mother Mary so that we have received fullness of grace like her, she was first to be full of grace.

When we have been baptized with fire by the Holy Spirit and all sin has been abolished in us, then we can have an immaculate Heart also. We have become the brides of Christ like Mary. No longer forsaken like Adam and Eve rather we are now delightful. We marry our Maker. We the land, have become espoused to God.

During Easter season, many are baptized and receive further sacraments. These sacraments continue to work throughout our lives. Every year we celebrate this Easter Joy. The harvest has begun and the reign of Christ is here.

> We are called to experience the Sacraments while fasting, so that our hearts and our lives can make room for growth in Jesus Christ. We also can prepare by being consecrated to Jesus through Mary every year. We can do it alone or with our brothers and sisters at church. (St. Louis de Montfort – True devotion to the Blessed Virgin or Preparation for the Reign of Jesus Christ). It works, keep coming back. The reason I say this is because the same people are coming every year and are persevering in true devotion. This exercise can lead all souls to heaven. There are also new people being consecrated every year.

"From a homily by Saint Ambrose, bishop – "Let Mary's soul be in each of you - Elizabeth was filled with the Holy Spirit after conceiving a son; Mary was filled before. "You are blessed," said Elizabeth, "because you have believed."

You too are blessed because you have heard and believed. The soul of every believer conceives and brings forth the Word of God and recognizes His works. Let Mary's soul be in each of you to glorify the Lord.

Let her spirit be in each of you to rejoice in the Lord. Christ has only one Mother in the flesh, but we all bring forth Christ by faith. Every soul free from contamination of sin and inviolate in its purity can receive the Word of God. Blessed are those who hear the Word of God and cherish it in their hearts." (Little Office of the Blessed Virgin Mary: Page 163).

So touching is the heart warming memories of the Virgin Mary…. of discovering the world through her eyes. We love you and appreciate all you do. Thank you for sharing your life with and in Christ with us and giving us the privilege of being part of Gods family. If we believe and trust in Jesus Christ everything God the Father gave Him, He also gives us.

"This pledge of new redemption and promise of eternal joy, prepared through ages   past, has dawned for us to day." (Divine Office page 185).

"O SING unto the Lord a new song; for he hath done marvelous things: his right hand, and his holy arm, hath gotten him the victory.

The Lord hath made known his salvation: his righteousness hath he openly shewed in the sight of the heathen.

He hath remembered his mercy and his truth toward the house of Israel: all the ends of the earth have seen the salvation of our God.

Make a joyful noise unto the Lord, all the earth: make a loud noise, and rejoice, and sing praise.

Sing unto the Lord with the harp; with the harp, and the voice of a psalm.

With trumpets and sound of cornet make a joyful noise before the Lord, the King.

Let the sea roar, and the fullness thereof; the world, and they that dwell therein.

Let the floods clap their hands; let the hills be joyful together

Before the Lord; for he cometh to judge the earth: with righteousness shall he judge the world, and the people with equity." (Psalm 98).

"Now from the heaven's descending, the Lord rebuilds Jerusalem and heals the broken hearted. Alleluia." (Divine Office page1585).

"We obtain Divine Mercy on the Day of Judgment." (Little Office of the Blessed Virgin page 98).

By the death of our Lord Jesus we have a clear revelation of God, for He was not like Moses, who would put a veil over his face. Life and immortality now brought to light, and things that have been hidden since the foundation of the world are displayed in Him.

Mother Eugenia was visited by God the Father and He shared with her some very important good news, and I, would like to share with you also. The name of her book is "God speaks to His Children". This is some of what she wrote pertaining to her book.

The three gifts that God the Father wishes to receive in homage from man, so that He may always be merciful and good even towards the most hardened sinners. "Honor me by establishing a feast in my honor and serving me." (Page 34). "I desire that one day, or at lest a Sunday, be dedicated to honoring me in a special way under the title of Father of all mankind. For this feast I would like a mass and Office, it is not difficult to find the texts in the Holy Scriptures. If you prefer to offer me this special devotion on a Sunday, I choose the first Sunday of August. If you prefer a weekday, I would like it to be always the seventh day of that same month." (Pages 34, 35 and 36).

"I come among you in two ways – the cross and the Eucharist!" (Page 25). "I also want to show you that I come among you through My Holy Spirit." (Page25).

"No one has yet understood the infinite desire of My divine paternal heart to be known, loved and honored by all men, the just and the sinful. (Page 26) "My heaven is on earth with you all, O men! Yes, it is on earth and in your souls that I look for my happiness and my joy." (Page 37). So by giving our Father the homage that He wishes we are pleasing Him. We are able to conceive or receive all the promises He has given us through His Son. When the coming of our Savior Jesus Christ is revealed to the living, and the dead they can be given everlasting life, in the here and now and forever more.

"The Lord does not want us to perish. He wants all the living to understand the infinite desire of His divine paternal heart. Loved and honored by all men, the just and the sinful. I have already told you that I want you to enjoy eternal happiness even here, on earth, but you still have not understood the real meaning of what I said. It is this: If you love me and call me by the sweet name of Father, you will begin to live here and now, in the love and the trust which will make you happy in eternity and which you will sing in heaven in the company of the elect. Is this not a foretaste of the happiness of heaven, which will last forever?"(Page 30).

Come, oh Holy Spirit, Fill the hearts of the Faithful and enkindle in them the fire of your love. Send forth you're Spirit and they will be created and they shall renew the face of the earth

The true precious love we can encounter from the Annunciation to Pentecost is available to all with and in Jesus Christ through the Holy Spirit in God's Almighty Power. I am a true witness of this love of Jesus Christ Crucified and God's Almighty Power. I am also a very grateful witness of Jesus Christ's Divine Mercy. He came from heaven into darkness and brought me into the light of his love and asked me to be His Bride. I know what I was and I know who I am now, the difference is like night and day. Miracles still happen. I am proof. Thank you for allowing me to share with you.

Please allow God to Bless You.

Your loving sister and mom, Cathryn Lucille Easley
P.S. Tomorrow is Pentecost May 23rd, 2010.

Chapter 4

June 6th 2010 Feast of the most Holy body and blood of Christ

I was in Durango, Colorado, doing time for a crime I had committed. While I was fasting and praying in the year 1988 when the Father drew me to Him in a dream, I was very upset because I did not understand what was going on pertaining to my vision of Jesus Christ and Billy my boyfriend.

The first thing I heard was: "who wants to go to earth and be Billy's girl friend." I felt my heart respond and I said: "I do." At that moment the Father drew me to Him. The sky and earth could not be seen. The only think I could see was our Father.

It felt as if I was only spirit. I could not see myself. But at the same time, I could sense that there were people or spirits there also.

When God the father said who wants to go to earth and be Billy's girl friend it also felt like I had been sleeping or in a state of rest in heaven, because I could not remember anything, past, present, or future. All I knew was at that moment God the Father was speaking to me.

He was speaking to me as if I hadn't been born yet. He explained to me some of the things that would happen before I would meet Billy. They were very beautiful but also very sad. I would meet someone else first and have two sons but that relationship wouldn't work out. I remember being very sad and crying very hard. Then He said I would meet Billy and that we would be very much in love, but by then I was crying so hard that it was hard for me to be happy about what He was saying. Then He said in the end you will not like it very much.

Then God the Father showed me the earth, and in front of the earth was Billy's face and the face of Christ that was in my vision, they look exactly the same He had a very angry look, although it did help me calm down. Then our Father told me that I would have to wait a short amount of time before all this would take place. And it felt like God the Father moved me from where I was with Him to a quiet place of rest. When I realized I was in my jail cell again I did remember the whole experience.

And some of the things that God the Father told me in my dream before I was born had already happened.

My mind, my body, my soul and spirit were put at ease. I went from woe is me to praising God. I realized how much God loves us and that by fasting and praying God draws us to Him. What was very interesting was that God the Father in my dream looked just like Ron Miller a man I had meet in Farmington, New Mexico. And later I saw a picture of Saint Vincent de Paul and God the Father resembles him a lot also.

I would really like to explain how I felt when the veil was lifted and I remembered the vision I had had, pertaining to Jesus Christ walking out of the clouds to me. I had the vision first and then the dream, from the Author of Life, God the Father of all mankind.

Brothers and Sisters when you come face to face with our Lord Jesus Christ, whether its in a vision or not you know who He is, and He makes it very clear that He knows you also. Then when He comes to earth to save you as the Son of Man, and you recognize Him, you are filled with a lot of emotions especially if you're not prepared. I myself was not prepared. I was in a major state of sin and very unlawful. The worst of sinners and very lost was I. So Jesus Christ was revealed to me in a vision and then manifested in my husband Billy, and God the Father was revealed in a dream and then manifested in my friend Ron Miller. They both spoke with authority in my vision and dream. But when manifested as my friend and boyfriend they appeared to be just that.

It took me a long time to realize what a horrible person I was. And that the works of my hands were abominations and that if left to myself I would of destroyed the earth. All of this was lived in the name of fun and happiness.

Oh, how I was deceived by my own lies! Each lie I told dug my hole deeper and deeper. I was in the end so deep in the earth, that I was doing the work of the anti-Christ – the beast – the devil - Satan himself. There was nowhere to go. I was stuck. This is what the great deceiver told me.

Praise God for the mustard seed of faith, which produced in me the strength to ask for help. So the day of fulfillment came to me and Jesus Christ came to me through the word of God: and while I was reading scripture, word for word, He taught me why He came and died and was resurrected and then ascended to His Throne.

Through His death He was able to go through the earth to where I was and bring me back redeemed. I was bathed in the blood of Jesus Christ Crucified with God's Almighty Power. What joy I have in my heart. I am a true witness of His Divine Mercy.

And it keeps getting better because I died to sin and experienced spiritual death with Jesus Christ' death in Gods Almighty Power, I was resurrected from spiritual death with and in Jesus and ascended to His Throne as one in His body and as one in His Spirit, to continue in spiritual life reigning with and in Jesus, Mary and Joseph, and all the saints world without end, in the new heaven and new earth.

So I find it very pleasing and beautiful in this state of grace where heaven and earth come together and we are building the kingdom of God on earth as it is in heaven. God is the father of those in heaven and earth; he does not want any of His children to perish, no matter how bad we have been. The gift of life is there being offered 24/7. We need to learn to surrender and submit before we destroy all that is truly dear to us and His kingdom, in Jesus name, Amen.

So what was revealed to me, in the vision and the dream did take place. The good and the bad. God the Father was right in the revelation, that in the end I would not like it. But He made everything better by sending His Son to redeem me, so that I could help build His kingdom on earth with the saints. Praise to you dear Father, Son and Holy Spirit. I love you because you loved me first. You showed me how to love myself so I could love my neighbor. And most of all I love thee.

I have all the support of the saints and martyrs, because of the blood they shed for us, and for the Word of God. They are so beautiful, and so glorious to behold. My body is truly in a state of chills.

I want to thank all the martyrs and saints, and tell you how grateful I am for everything you have done and continue to do for me and all God's children. I truly do love you all, and I feel very privileged to know you. Your work in the new heaven and new earth is seen by me by the grace of God.

So if it is the will of our Father that we dwell with Him in heavenly places while living in the new heaven and new earth, why not do so and be Holy and pleasing before our Father?

NOTE: To parents we can teach our children about our Lord Jesus Christ and God's Almighty Power and His Kingdom, but there can come a day when we have to let go and let God do His work, and trust that the Spirit of Truth will come and they will have the Freedom to exercise their Faith and we can look forward to the day when they can be glorifying God in His Kingdom. But in the mean time's, I say mean time's because like most kids they think they know everything and we know nothing, so I call that the mean time's. Thank God all things can be solemnly given to the Trinity and to our Mother in Heaven. May we all be one and be at peace with one another, in Jesus Christ name, Amen.   IMIRUI2 + I am one are you one too?

Forgiveness plays a very important role for those that want to draw close to our Lord. He sets a very good example for us; forgive them Father for they know not what they do. We also need to forgive those that have trespassed against us, so that we won't be led into temptation. There are a lot of horrible things going on in the world and even in our own homes. We need to take one step at a time and start within ourselves, we have no control over what other people say or do, only ourselves. So that makes things a bit easier.

Please allow the fire to destroy all the bad feelings that we have inside of us towards someone or ourselves. If we retain them, they will hold us back. They are the fruit of Satan. And he loves company. When we allow the fire to do its work, we will know we are completely free. Everyone has tribulations in his or her life some more than others. And not everyone's is the same.

Jesus Christ never changes. He is always waiting for us his children to turn to Him so He can heal us. It might not be easy, but it can be done, and we will be so glad that we did. We will rise above it all and not look back. The baptism of fire purifies the world within us. And it enables us to become a new creation. We can allow the spirit to do its work in us as the Father wills. That's when heaven and earth meet. The two dimensions become one in Jesus through the Holy Spirit in God's Almighty Power. (Thy kingdom come thy will be done on earth as it is in heaven). So this explains also why I see those in heaven on earth doing God's will.

In regard to the year 2012: when some people think the world is going to end. If it be God's will this scroll will be in circulation to enlighten my brothers and sisters. That the world and the evil that it contains is within us! Do not be afraid. Prepare yourselves. Allow the Spirit and fire to do its work in each of us individually, spiritually and physically. That we may be purified by the baptism of fire, that the root of evil will be destroyed in each of us individually. Allow Mary into your hearts, follow her virtues; and she can lead us to Jesus and He will lead us to heaven, where God the Father dwells; and Jesus Christ will present us to our Father spotless. This is what I believe we were created for. To know God, and to love God, to be with and in God and to be a servant of God: in heaven on earth. There is no reason to hang around in limbo doing nothing, or in purgatory. The definition of limbo is "the abode of souls excluded from the full blessedness of the beatific vision, but not suffering any other punishment. They enjoy the happiness that would have been human destiny if humans had not been elevated to the supernatural order." (Modern Catholic Dictionary by John A. Hardon, S.J. page 319).

The definition of Purgatory: "The place or condition in which the souls of the just are purified after death and before they can enter heaven. They may be purified of the quilt of their venial sins, as in this life, by an act of contrition deriving from charity and performed with the help of grace. This sorrow does not, however, affect the punishment for sins, because in the next world there is no longer any possibility of merit. The souls are certainly purified by atoning for the temporal punishments due to sin by their willing acceptance of suffering imposed by God. The sufferings in purgatory are not the same for all, but proportioned to each person's degree of sinfulness. Moreover, these sufferings can be lessened in duration and intensity through the prayers and good works of the faithful on earth. Nor are the pains incompatible with great peace and joy, since the poor souls deeply love God and are sure they will reach heaven. As members of the Church Suffering, the souls in purgatory can intercede for the persons on earth, who are therefore encouraged to invoke their aid. Purgatory will not continue after the general judgment, but its duration for any particular soul continues until it is free from all guilt and punishment. Immediately on purification the soul is assumed into heaven." (Etym. Latin purgation, cleansing, purifying"). (Modern Catholic Dictionary by John A. Hardon, S.J.). Jesus wants us all to experience purgatory before we physically die that we might be with and in Him now. We should experience great remorse for our sins for what they cost our Savior. We don't need to stay in that state forever; we can acknowledge what Jesus has done for us and move on. The next place that we experience is either heaven or Hell either ascending to the Throne or condemning our selves. If we love Jesus and the things of God we can pick up our Bible, read and pray for wisdom and understanding. Ask God in the name of Jesus Christ to please send the Spirit of truth. And don't give up. If we do not reflect all that Jesus is, it is to our own shame.

It has taken me twenty five years and I am forty nine years old now. To start to understand, but I am moving forward through the Holy Spirit with and in Jesus Christ through God's Almighty Power, Praise God. I had to read the Bible a lot and still do, devotionals help and prayers are also very important for us. It takes work on our part if we want to be part of Gods kingdom. That Kingdom of God' truly does exist, and when we focus on the Word of God it can be manifested in us. I do testify to that. I also have a lot of help from the Saints. Though they have passed and gone to heaven, they are still interceding for us, and they are alive and dwell among us in heavenly places. This is a foreshadow of the things to come, for all the faithful that believe in the promises of Christ This foreshowing of the interceding of the saints can be manifested during our life time, if we would give them the time of day. When you look beyond this world into the next you can see them, they are so beautiful and bright. And this is truly being revealed for our own well being. God can raise us up and we can live with the angels, saints and

Jesus in heavenly places, all of us one in Jesus Christ his body, the church. The Trinity and Unity are proper to God. Although there is a wall that separates the two dimensions which is heaven and earth. Dig a hole, (search the scriptures) and we can see the other side. And if we tear the wall down we can pass over to the other side as we will. When we dwell in heaven on earth we are experiencing two dimensions at the same time.

We know that if we believe in and accept Christ as our savior, we are saved. But if we stay in that state and do nothing more, we can wait till we physically die to hope to go to heaven. Instead we can live perpetually with and in Jesus Christ as the members of His body in heaven on earth whether we are living or dead. All the promises of Christ are attainable for the living and the dead. So I highly recommend working hard and running the race and being victorious in the here and now, and forever more.

We the living can experience all God the Father has to offer. It can be a wonderful feeling knowing we are pleasing our Father and that Jesus did not suffer and die in vain, nor the Martyrs, that we the living can be moving in the right direction. Please do not be idol. Please seek the kingdom of God. I am praying that we all can be reunited through the Holy Spirit in heaven on earth that we obtain the great gift being offered through Jesus Christ Crucified in God's Almighty Power. That all of us can live in the new heaven and new earth and unite in oneness in mind, body, soul and spirit with and in Jesus Christ under God indivisibly with Liberty and Justice for all, in the here and now and forever more in Jesus precious name Amen.

Oh Lord, teach us to be humble down on our knees. Teach us how to please.

When we listen to what our Mother Mary has been saying through apparitions, we will learn that we have been told to pray, repent, fast, and have a conversion of our heart. When we experience this it is through our mind, body, soul and spirit, through the Holy Spirit with and in Jesus Christ Crucified and with the exercise of God's Almighty Power.

We have to allow the spirit of fire to do its work in us as is described in the book of Revelations regarding the destruction of the world (which is us, individually).

We can allow the fire of God's love to melt our cold, cold hearts. While fasting we can give up something we like doing, so as to make room for Jesus.

What's really cool is when I learned I didn't have to be right all the time. That's when I was able to start learning, and listening to others. This enabled me to be able to see and hear better. It also gave me understanding and compassion for others. Having to be right all the time is a form of greed, stubbornness and pride. Being able to see and hear leads to peace within us. Our Father cannot abide in hearts that are unclean. So when we learn to leave behind this behavior, that's when we can be free to follow Jesus Christ. Guess what? We are becoming teachable and we only want to seek the truth. Our Lord promises freedom, happiness and peace.

"In your justice give us life, Father. Do not allow greed to possess us but incline our hearts to your commands. Give us understanding to know your law and direct us according to your will." (Divine Office page 1022).

The Holy Spirit is teaching us to trust our Lord. When we learn to trust Jesus, we begin to show integrity. It is becoming a mutual love. Honesty is so important there is never a good reason to lie to yourself or someone. If we have to lie to get something that we want, we truly don't need it. If we have to steal something, we truly never needed it, we are only deceiving ourselves, and we will have to live with the consequences.

Our Lord provides for us, his grace is sufficient. Be content, be grateful for everything we have been given. A good attitude is a very grateful one.

We also need to learn not to knock people down, treat everyone with kindness and love, and appreciate everyone equally. This is what I call goodwill towards all. So now we can see how much fruit comes from being humble. When we have become humble enough to seek help, then we start seeing and hearing better the confusion seems to dissolve. We can hear things clearly and we can see with the light of truth. And everything is beginning to be made straight and smooth. This is where we can encounter bliss. No more warring. Our Mother Mary's heart will triumph. Our conversion leads to perfect sight and perfect hearing. Our Mother in heaven wants all her children to be able to see and hear again. And she wants her children to have everlasting life in the here and now and forever more and to live happily ever after.

"To the God who gives us the joy of praising him this morning, and who strengthens our hope, let us pray: Hear us, O Lord, for the glory of your name. We thank you, God and Father of Jesus our Savior, - for the knowledge and immortality you have given us through him. Make us humble of heart, - help us to serve one another out of reverence for Christ. Pour out your Spirit on us, your servants, - make us sincere in our love for each other. You instructed man to labor and to exercise dominion over the earth, - may our work honor you and sanctify our brothers and sisters." (Divine Office pages 952 and 953).

In her book Father of all mankind, Mother Eugenia states. "The Father of all Mankind wants us to know that we have a father, who, having created us, wants to give us treasures He possesses. And above all, to tell us that He thinks of us, and He loves us, and wants to give us eternal happiness."

May God the Father Bless us all and give us all perfect hearing and perfect vision in Jesus Christ's name. All through our Mother Mary's hands may we all glorify our Father and Son and Holy Spirit: as it was in the beginning, is now, and will be forever. Amen. We can give all glory and honor and praise to the Trinity forever more. Amen.

By Jesus Christ great sacrifice He has opened Heaven on earth to everyone not just the Jews, when we live with and in the spirit of truth all denominations are welcome, Our Father is the Father of all mankind.

Chapter 5

July 16, 2010   Feast of our Lady of Mount Carmel

I want to explain what happened to me and why I say I dwell in heaven on earth with the Holy Family and the saints. When the old world was within me, or I should say us, is destroyed by the baptism of fire through the Holy spirit by God Almighty and Jesus Christ Crucified, the new heaven and new earth came down from heaven. And I became the bride of Jesus Christ in the New Jerusalem and the City of God dwells within me and all around me. And this is also where the Trinity dwells. I was no longer forsaken but have become delightful. And many things were and are revealed to me about His Kingdom. God has revealed to me that all the people that have fallen asleep in death and that have been given life in heaven from Adam and Eve until now dwell in the new heaven and new earth.

What I am saying is that we the living don't have to only wait till we fall asleep, to go to Heaven. That in the end when Christ comes for the living and the dead and everything has been restored by Jesus Christ in God's Almighty Power then there can be life in heaven on earth! That we the living can find life, happiness and peace in the new heaven and new earth through Jesus Christ Crucified in God's Almighty Power. That we the living can say "yes," "come Lord Jesus" and ask for His Divine mercy and we can be set free by our Savior Jesus Christ through the Holy Spirit in God's Almighty Power. And we can die to sin and experience a spiritual death, because we all are sinners, and we need our Fathers Almighty Power and Jesus Christ Crucified to restore us to the way we were in the beginning: The Theology of Justification states "the process of a sinner becoming justified or made right with God as defined by the Council of Trent" "Justification is the change from the condition in which a person is born as a child of the first Adam into a state of grace and adoption among the children of God through the Second Adam, Jesus Christ our Savior" (Denzinger 1524). On the negative side, justification is a true removal of sin, and not merely having one's sins ignored or no longer held against the sinner by God. On the positive side it is the supernatural sanctification and renewal of a person who thus becomes holy and pleasing to God and an heir of heaven. The Catholic Church identifies five elements of justification, which collectively define its full meaning. The primary purpose of justification is the honor of God and of Christ; its secondary purpose is the eternal life of mankind. The main efficient cause or agent is the mercy of God; the main instrumental cause is the sacrament of baptism, which is called the "sacrament of baptism, which is called the "sacrament of faith" to spell out the necessity of faith for salvation. And that which constitutes justification or its essence is the justice of God, "not by which He is just Himself, but by which He makes us just," namely sanctifying grace. Depending on the sins from which a person is to be delivered, there are different kinds of justification. An infant is justified by baptism and the faith of the one who requests or confers the sacrament. Adults are justified for the first time either by personal faith, sorrow for sin and baptism, or by the perfect love of God, which is at least on implicit baptism of desire. Adults who have sinned gravely after being justified can receive justification by sacramental absolution or perfect contrition for their sins." (Modern Catholic Dictionary by John A. Hardon S.J. pages 302 and 302). Our Lord cannot abide with unclean spirits. Jesus Christ in God's Almighty Power sends the Holy spirit to baptize us with water, which washes away our sins. And the fire destroys the old world that contained mortal sin and death (evil) in us individually and personally, so that God can give us a new glorious spiritual life with Him and in Him, and we can ascend to the Throne with and in Jesus Christ to the new heaven and new earth which is heaven on earth. "I would like to share what the Summa Theologiae says about spiritual death and baptism, by Thomas Aquinas. Baptism is spiritual birth, a change from spiritual death to spiritual life, represented as a washing: on both counts it is appropriate for someone conscious of fatal sin to approach baptism. But in this sacrament man takes into himself Christ, represented as spiritual nourishment, and this is not appropriate for one dead in sin." (Summa Theologiae page 585). The definition of Spiritual Death is: "The state of the soul in mortal sin, based on the analogy with BODILY DEATH. Just as a physical body may be not only ill or suffer injury, but cease to live. It is, therefore, spiritually dead because it is no longer united with God, who gives it supernatural life, even as a body is dead on separation from its animating principle, which is the soul. While still on earth, this union with God is both a possession and a movement.

We possess him by grace and in faith, and we are moving toward him in the beatific vision of glory. When persons sin mortally, they are twice dead: once because they lose the gift of divine life they formerly had, and once again because they are no longer moving toward the consummation of that life in heaven.

Mortal sins are no longer remissible by any power within the soul itself, much as the human body, once dead, cannot be brought back to life except by a special intervention of God. In Patristic literature the restoration is compared with the resuscitation of Lazarus. The exercise of Almighty power in either case is the same. "Everyone who sins, dies," says St. Augustine. Only the Lord, "by his great grace and great mercy raises souls to life again, that we may not die eternally." (Modern Catholic Dictionary by John A. Hardon, S.J. Page 515) Only infinite mercy can reconcile the grave sinner." (In Joannis Evangelium, 49). (Once again loud thunder and lightning bolts all around us and rain from heaven we have lost all power. Almighty God in His great power is purifying the world, us. Praise God). Dear brothers and sisters when we allow the Holy Spirit to do its work in us fully, we can become a new creation with and in Christ Jesus Himself. And we with an idea of the love of God can share in that love in the present moment, and forever. Remember, we have become God's adopted children, and Jesus and God the Father are offering us eternal life now and after death, so that we can live as God lives. This is why I say my home is made by our Father's creating hand, tiss heaven on earth and this most holy and precious gift is being offered to all unbelievers and sinners that would have a conversion of heart and accept and believe. We can move our mind, body, soul and spirit from the darkness of sin and eternal death to the light of pure eternal life. We can allow the Spirit of Truth to remove the darkness from us. I believe after we physically die Jesus is standing at the gates of hell still offering a better way to unbelievers and sinners. These people at that moment may also accept and believe and can be given heaven. Jesus knows that these people were deceived by the devil and it is completely against Jesus' nature to allow these poor souls to inter into hell because they did not hear the Word. Only the souls that were with Lucifer will go to hell.

When we are conceived by our parents, we are truly a blessing and a gift from our Father in heaven, and we are still in a state of sleep, and as baby's we can be washed with holy water and be baptized to remove the stain of original sin, so no longer are we barred from the beatific vision, and as we grow we can grow in holiness. Then we come to an age where we become accountable and we begin our journey, we can unite with the Catholic Church and we can live in the sacraments, so in this way we can be consecrated to the Lord. We can find ourselves in travail due to saying "yes," "come Lord Jesus," and because of our Baptism we know original sin has been removed through Almighty Power and Jesus Christ Crucified through the Holy Spirit of God, so in this way when Christ comes and we conceive the Holy

Spirit we can give birth to Jesus in us without sin, so in this way we are becoming more like our Mother Mary.

We have conceived the Holy Spirit like the Virgin Mary and we also can be full of grace. So now we have a conception, and the baby Jesus is growing in side of us and when the time of fulfillment has arrived we can give birth to Jesus in us spiritually and then when it is time for us to die to sin we can find ourselves at the foot of the cross in Jerusalem with Jesus and Mary and we can unite our spiritual death with Mary and with Jesus Christ.

Jesus and Mary suffered immensely, so in this way we can also suffer immensely at our spiritual death or our physical death when we are uniting as one in the body and in the spirit. So through this suffering we have united with them, we are no longer living in the old world of flesh rather we are living through the Holy Spirit in Christ' body we have truly experienced spiritual death and or physical death with and in Jesus Christ Crucified and through the great gift of God's Almighty Power.

We the living and the dead can be resurrected from spiritual death and or physical death and we can be born again and or reborn and we can be resurrected united as one in Jesus Christ no longer I, but you Lord. All the things of the earth and the old world we have left behind, all the things that pertain to us are dead. Spiritually and physically we are given a glorified body which is Jesus Christ body, and we can live with and in it, and in this way we have become the members of His Holy Body.

Now that we the living and the dead are given a new spiritual life with and in Jesus Christ in God's Almighty Power we are no longer citizens of the earth. But rather we have become citizens of the new heaven and new earth with and in our Lord, in the New Jerusalem. So in this way we can be living the gospel and we can reach heaven on earth while living in this live and or in the life to come.

Now that we realize that we the living and the dead can dwell in heaven on earth which is the new heaven and new earth and that we can see our loved ones that have gone to heaven and also angles and the saints. We can see them glorifying our Lord, we can also see them interceding for the living and the dead. And we can be in communion with them, and this is why our Lord had to suffer so and die. So that Jesus Christ could save all mankind from eternal death and eternal damnation. So in this way Jesus could give us everlasting life with Him and in Him, in heaven on earth.

We perpetually live in this state of life knowing that we can never die eternally, but we do realize that our time here on earth is short; we also know that we dwell in heaven on earth forever, and we also know that this is His Kingdom and that His Kingdom is not of the world. God's Kingdom is spirit and truth.

So when our days are spent in the new heaven and new earth and our bodies are wore out, we know we must return to God the same way we came, so God the Father gives us rest and we fall asleep in death still living as members of Jesus Christ' body forever in heaven on earth. So in this way the Trinity has truly bestowed a blessing upon us with a privilege that we cannot earn, it is freely given and we can freely accept.

This is not word for word pertaining to sacred scripture but it does contain the Truth that we can find in the Holy Bible pertaining to the living and the dead. And we can realize that we don't have to wait only on physical death to enter into heaven on earth. But that Jesus Christ is waiting 4 us to say "yes," "Come Lord Jesus."

So in this way if we follow the Word of God and all its symbols and metaphors we can manifest the word of God in our lives, we can do this through our sacraments which can lead us to Spiritual Death with and in Jesus Christ Crucified and in God's Almighty Power. So in this way in our spiritual and or our physical existence we can also have experienced all that God the Father and His Son through the Holy Spirit wants to give His children.

Like I said we all will fall asleep or rather experience death when our life comes to and end. And those that are sleeping in the Lord do dwell in heaven on earth. We the living and the dead can experience the new heaven and new earth.

And this is a gift from God and His Son Jesus through the Holy Spirit. And a promise of theirs to us, that when Jesus returns in the end, he will make all things new. And this new state of life can be heaven on earth for the living and the dead that are experiencing spiritual death, and or physical death. They can be born again and or reborn and they can be raised up to a new spiritual life through Jesus Christ Crucified with God's Almighty Power.

Is this not a form of heaven on earth? The new heaven and new earth also move us to a higher consciousness which enables us to become more. And this is also good in Gods eyes, because in this way we are still growing spiritually. And the good news is Jesus comes for all. No one has to be left 4 dead.

Whenever Christ spoke of people in regard to being dead he referred to them as sleeping not dead. When we unite our spiritual death and or our physical death with and in Jesus Christ's death it is the only time we can encounter eternal death, (if we say "no" to Jesus Christ will we suffer with eternal death?) we can experience this with Jesus Christ at His Crucifixion. But we know that by Jesus Christ's death we are not under the old law. The old law was abolished under Jesus Christ Crucified pertaining to death and His ascension into heaven. We can accept the gift of grace and charity and be restored to everlasting life with Him and in Him in heaven on earth.

We the living and the dead can be resurrected from spiritual death and or physical death that we have or will incur when our life has ended as we know it, so that we can return to our natural state which is heaven on earth, and we can be reconciled to God through the Holy Spirit and Jesus Christ. So that we can walk with God in Paradise in His kingdom, and His kingdom is in the new heaven and new earth.

And this is how we can continue to dwell in heaven on earth after spiritual death and physical death. And this is how those that are living and those that are dead can be resurrected and be born again and or reborn to a new spiritual life with and in Jesus Christ Crucified in God's Almighty Power in the here and now and or in the life to come.

In the new heaven and new earth we find that the people there never die, and they dwell there with us and we realize that we are immortal, spiritual beings also. Like Our Savior Jesus Christ and His Mother world without end. There is no fear of death there! Oh, death where is your sting?

The curse of eternal death and eternal damnation no longer has power over the living and the dead, because we know we can be born again and or reborn without sin and we can be given everlasting life, through the Holy Spirit with and in Jesus Christ Crucified in God's Almighty Power. What joy and rejoicing we have within us, all of us living in the body of Jesus Christ together in heaven on earth. We His grateful children give all glory to God on High. No longer are we lost, we have been found by our Savior Jesus Christ! And we have been made worthy by Jesus Christ's precious body and blood. His body and blood is our promise and our atonement, all through God's Almighty Power from Heaven. We the living and the dead have been blessed with much love, kindness and compassion from the Ones that really care about our souls.

We all will fall asleep in the Lord at the end of our life, yet we the living and the dead know we will never eternally die; we are living in our Lord Jesus Christ we are the members of His Holy body whether awake or asleep. But for those still awake, there is so much out there to reap and enjoy while you still have time. Thank you, loving Trinity for sharing your death and life and your truth with me, and allowing me to share with my brothers and sisters in Jesus Christ. I believe God is gathering His people into His True Church where the true Kingdom is. And this is where we hope our loved ones go.

We have truly been blessed with abundance from our Father and His Son Jesus Christ through the Holy Spirit. After Christ comes and we the living and the dead are resurrected and united in Jesus Christ's glorified body we are immortal beings moving in the spirit to our consummation. "I believe in God, I have Faith in Jesus Christ and I Trust in the Holy Spirit. We need to have all 3 things to have Love, God is Love." (Billy Easley).

Once again we find ourselves becoming more like our Mother Mary and the things of heaven and of God are all happening within us and all around us. I cannot and would not try to explain everything of God. But my desire is to show that there is heaven on earth for the living and the dead and that we don't have to wait only on the sleep of death to inherit heaven, but we have to say "yes," "Come Lord Jesus" and be baptized and we can be justified and ask for our Father's Divine Mercy and we can experience spiritual death through the Holy Spirit with and in Jesus Christ Crucified. Almighty Power has to occur and then fire from God. This fire is what the Holy Spirit baptizes us with and it destroys the root of evil in us the world. In which we inherited from Adam and Eve and our own trespasses. Only then are we capable of conceiving the word of God without sin. And in this Way we are becoming more like our Mother Mary. Conceiving: with out sin. We like Mary can say "yes," "Come Lord Jesus" The romance can begin and we can conceive the Holy Spirit in our mind, body, soul and spirit like Mary, we can have a conception and we can give birth to the Word in us. We can be born again and or reborn this is also what we call regenerated without sin. We can experience spiritual death with Jesus Christ Crucified in God's Almighty Power and the old world of sin and evil can be destroyed spiritually by the baptism of fire and we can be resurrected from our spiritual death and or our physical death and we can continue to live with and in Jesus Christ's body in our mind, body, soul and spirit all by grace and our faith and deeds done in Jesus Christ in God's Almighty Power.

Our minds can become one in faith with Jesus Christ's. And the new heaven and new earth can come down from heaven and we can become the Bride's of Jesus Christ and we can live with and in Jesus with Joseph and Mary and all our loved ones, to be with God in heavenly places, world without end.

All this is happening within us the world. And because of this exercise we know that we the living and the dead have been blessed by the Trinity's Almighty Power, what a great blessing. And in this way the flock is given the way: Death, Life and Truth.

Both spiritual death and physical death with and in the Lord through the Holy Spirit in God's Almighty Power are a chain of events that can lead to the resurrection and living in heaven on earth. Are not these the steps that Jesus and Mary took? Of their own free will! I believe that if we stay on this path it will lead us in perfection and we will experience His promises and we will be given life everlasting in the new heaven and new earth.

"Yes," "Come Lord Jesus." 2. Conceive. 3. Conception. 4. Birth. 5. Death 6. Life. 7. Heaven. This is the gospel and it is sacred, we can conceive the Holy Spirit and receive these great blessings through the sacraments in the here and now, and forever more. With Jesus Christ Crucified, and the exercise of Almighty Power. In our spirituality all things are possible with God. Have you ever heard someone say something about seventh heaven? Perhaps this is what they were talking about.

"Make my joy complete by your unanimity, possessing the one love, united in spirit and ideals. Never act out of rivalry or conceit; rather, let all parties think humbly of others as superior to themselves, each of you looking to other's interests rather than his own. In everything you do, act without grumbling or arguing; prove yourselves innocent and straightforward, children of God beyond reproach in the midst of a twisted and depraved generation—among whom you shine like the stars in the sky while holding fast to the word of life. As I look to the Day of Christ, you give me cause to boast that I did not run the race in vain or work to no purpose." (Divine Office Page 919 Philippians 2:2-4, 14-16).

"God our Father, fountain and source of our salvation, may we proclaim your glory every day of our lives, that we may sing your praise for ever in heaven. We ask this through our Lord Jesus Christ, you Son, who lives, and reigns with you and the Holy Spirit, one God, forever and ever." (Divine Office Page 920).

This scroll was written to stand forever for all unbelievers and sinners whether living or dead, that if we do believe in the Second Coming of Jesus Christ. That we will and we can be taken to heaven if we are ready to accept and believe. Whether you the hearer believe what I say about my vision of Jesus Christ and Him walking out of the clouds to me is up to you, and I know it's hard to believe that Jesus Christ has manifest Himself through the Holy Spirit with and in my husband Billy, this is my reality and I love every moment of it. It would be for the good of all if the hearer could and would accept my reality that it would become your present reality now also. We are called to see Christ in all His children.

Because God is so beautiful I want to share with my brothers and sisters, everything that God has given me, so in this way if you believe that your relationship with the Lord is a personal one, and that your salvation is also personal, and when the time of His return occurs it is also personal, and that no one else is seeing what you are seeing or what you are hearing nor are they experiencing what you are all at the same time. Then I believe you are on the right path.

We the living and the dead in heaven on earth, in our spiritual lives know we can conceive the Holy Spirit without sin through the Holy Spirit baptizing us with water and fire through Jesus Christ Crucified in God's Almighty Power. We also know that we can not die eternally. So with this knowledge and wisdom we have been endowed with everlasting life in heaven on earth, thus eternal life. We also acknowledge that our human bodies are made of the earth, so that through the Holy Spirit our coming and goings are the works of your Almighty hand Father. In the beginning we were created in God's image. Adam and eve sinned. Now we experience through the Holy Spirit our spiritual death and our physical death through Jesus Christ Crucified in order for us to stay in a state of grace for all eternity, offered through God Almighty.

We can in our spiritual and physical existence reject eternal death and eternal damnation. And we can accept and believe in life everlasting with and in Jesus Christ through the Holy Spirit in God's Almighty Power. We do encounter spiritual death and physical death in this possession of Jesus Christ, this movement is all in the name of God Almighty. So in this way: tiss heaven on earth for the living and the dead. We that live in the Spirit of God Almighty, but yet also have earthly bodies know that when our time on earth is over we must return to the earth but yet we are still in heaven on earth.

"Jesus, Redeemer on earth. Because Christ also died once for sins, the Just for the unjust, that he might bring us to God. Put to death indeed in the flesh, he was brought to life in the spirit, in which also he went and preached to those spirits that were in prison. For to this end was the gospel preached even to the dead, that they may be judged indeed as men in flesh but may live as God lives in spirit." (My daily reading from the New Testament and daily mass book: Arrangement by Father Stedman Page 398. 1 Peter.3:18-19).

In the end, the living and the dead can be resurrected and can be born again and or reborn after all things have been restored personally and individually in us the world, then comes heaven on earth spiritually and physical and we are given everlasting life in God's kingdom with and in Jesus Christ with the Holy Ones, and also our loved ones. Death, life, and truth are being offered to all God's children that we may have freedom, happiness and peace in us throughout the world. This is what our Father and His Son through the Holy Spirit have done for us, the worst of sinner's in the here and now. I hope the hearer can imagine how grateful I am to be able to tell all my brothers and sisters how much God loves us. "The wilderness and the dry land shall be glad, the desert shall rejoice and blossom; like the crocus it shall blossom abundantly, and rejoice with joy and singing. The glory of Lebanon shall be given to it, the majesty of Carmel and Sharon. They shall see the glory of the Lord, the majesty of our God." (Isaiah 35:1-2).

The pictures in our book are a good example of our coming and going through the Holy Spirit here in heaven on earth all through God' loving creating hands. That heaven on earth does exist, and that we the living and the dead can be united in one body that of Jesus Christ's and Jesus Christ is the head of His body, and that we the living and the dead can live all together in the new heaven and new earth, forever more. That God's Universal Word and His eternal promises might be displayed in His Creation through Him, with Him, and in Him, creating spiritual creation through the Holy Spirit and Jesus Christ Crucified. MAY GOD BLESS YOU, I LOVE YOU ALL.

Chapter 6

July 21, 2010 Feast of St. Lawrence of Brindisi

Revelation itself, or what kind of vision and dream? – Private or Public? My vision and dream is all three. Private: because Jesus walked out of the clouds in a vision to me. Public: because it brings Jesus to all. I used Revealed Law to explain my vision and dream. Revelation itself in the since that God dwells among us through the Holy Spirit in heaven on earth. And that The Trinity also dwells in heaven on earth, and the Trinity is revealed through a vision and a dream and has been manifested to me, all three ways, which are Revelation itself, public and private.

On earth Jesus Christ is manifested in my husband Billy through the Holy Spirit. Also on earth God the Father is manifested in Ron Miller through the Holy Spirit. And in my dream God the Father was revealed to me in heaven. Jesus Christ in heaven is revealed to me through a vision. Jesus Christ is the great mediator and revealer of all Revelation. Our Lord Jesus spoke these words, that whoever has seen me has also seen my father.

When we are moving in the Spirit of Truth, we can draw from Sacred Scripture what was prophesied about the Second Coming of Jesus Christ. He will return to us the same way he left in the clouds. He left us as the risen and living spirit, "Jesus Christ," there was but a few people that witnessed Jesus Christ ascending to Heaven, yet all believers base their faith on their testimony and it is all by faith that we have this hope of Jesus Christ returning in the same way.

And this is why I am using human words to describe what has happened to me because of my vision and dream. Jesus truly walked out of the clouds to me in a vision and then in a glorious manifestation through the Holy Spirit in my husband Billy. So in this way we could say that he has returned to us through a vision and a dream and then also through a glorious manifestation and that the manifestation and the dream and also the vision are Revelation itself. And that the Trinity does dwell among us in the new heaven and new earth and this Promised Land does exist, but like I said before it is not of this world. God's kingdom can be within each and every one of His children; if we would open the door to our hearts and our lives and invite Jesus in to stay.

If we are of the world we will reap the things of the world, and they all lead to death. But if we are of the Spirit we will reap the things of heaven, which is everlasting life. When we try to make sense of it and we use worldly ideals to understand Gods Kingdom we can be left 4 dead. (Death is a stage 5 in our spirituality 7 is Heaven) Rather, we can allow the Holy Spirit and God's Almighty Power to exercise us the world through Jesus Christ Crucified. And in this way the world can be transformed and it can become part of Gods Kingdom and in this Kingdom God has many mansions and all of this is happening within us and all around the world all at different times and places. One thing for sure when Jesus Christ comes there is no mistaking it. Because this possession of Jesus Christ is so large and the movement in the Holy Spirit, is so wide there is no way I could explain it all. But the activity that I do see is truly amazing, so many things going on through the Holy Spirit pertaining to the Word of God, and His kingdom. Jesus' kingdom within me is overflowing with gratitude and God's Almighty Power. So by explaining it this way we can see that it's all within us and that when Jesus Christ returns it's a personal relationship that is being built upon Rock. I my self was also brought up to believe that in the Second Coming of Christ everyone would see Jesus in the clouds returning all at the same time. But God has revealed otherwise to me.

Let me explain what I mean by left 4 dead, this is the people that are living spiritually dead due to sin and evil in side of them. They stay in that state and do nothing about it. "Mortal Sin, An actual sin that destroys sanctifying grace and causes the supernatural death of the soul. Mortal sin is a turning away from God because of a seriously inordinate adherence to creatures that causes grave injury to a person's rational nature and to the social order, and deprives the sinner of a right to heaven.

The terms mortal, deadly, grave, and serious applied to sin are synonyms, each with a slightly different implication. Mortal and deadly focus on the effects in the sinner, namely deprivation of the state of friendship with God; grave and serious refer to the importance of the matter in which a person offends God. But the Church never distinguishes among these terms as though they represented different kinds of sins. There is only one recognized correlative to mortal sin, and that is venial sin, which offends against God but does not cause the loss of one's state of grace". (Etym. Latin mors, death.)   (Modern Catholic Dictionary John A. Hardon, S.J.). So the unbelievers and sinners live their life without being reconciled to God, they haven't united as one in the body through the spirit nor have they ascended to the throne with and in Jesus Christ through the Holy Spirit in God's Almighty Power. So that leaves them left 4 dead. The definition - of Original Sin is. "Either the sin committed by Adam as the head of the human race, or the sin he passed onto his posterity with which every human being, with the certain exception of Christ and his Mother, is conceived and born. The sin of Adam is called originating original sin (originale originans); that of his descendants is originated original sin (originale originatum). Adams's sin was personal and grave, and it affected human nature. It was personal because he freely committed it; it was grave because God imposed a serious obligation; and it affected the whole human race by depriving his progeny of the supernatural life and preternatural gifts they would have possessed on entering the world had Adam not sinned. Original sin in his descendants is personal only in the sense that the children of Adam are each personally affected, but not personal as though they had voluntarily chosen to commit the sin; it is grave in the sense that it debars a person from the beatific vision, but not grave in condemning one to hell; and it is natural only in that all human nature, except for divine intervention, has it and can have it removed only by supernatural means." (Modern Catholic Dictionary John A, Hardon, S.J. Page 395). And this is why we the living and the dead (unbelievers and sinners) need Jesus Christ Crucified in God's Almighty Power through the Holy Spirit to intervene and use supernatural means to restore us to our original state as it was in the beginning before Adam and Eve sinned. Where we the living and the dead can live forever in everlasting happiness and peace with and in God in His Kingdom which is heaven on earth, and this is where the new heaven and new earth can be for all God's children. That unbelievers and sinners may convert, accept and believe! This is why we the living have to spiritually die to sin and experience spiritual death with and in Jesus Christ Crucified in God's Almighty Power through the Holy Spirit so we can be reconciled to God through our Savior and God's Son Jesus Christ. And this is why we the living and the dead have to experience physical death, so Jesus Christ Crucified in God's Almighty Power through the Holy Spirit can spiritually and physically resurrect us from spiritual and physical death to a new spiritual life in heaven on earth, we can be born again and or reborn through our spiritual and our physical existence they go hand in hand with Jesus Christ's divine and human nature. So in this way we are always living in a state of grace offered through Jesus Christ Crucified all in God's Almighty Power through the Holy Spirit. So when we the living experience physical death we know we are sleeping in the Lord and that we are members of His Holy Body whether asleep or awake, and we know we must return to the earth. When we are resurrected from the dead and we are born again we are woken from our sleep. When we the living through the Holy Spirit die to sin and experience spiritual death with and in Jesus Christ' death, we are united in His spirit and we are resurrected with and in Jesus Christ in God's Almighty Power, thus we are reborn and given a new spiritual life with and in Jesus Christ Crucified in God's Almighty Power. We the living know that this is the new heaven and new earth, and this is what we call the New Israel, these two places we call home sweet home. And yes animals do live in heaven on earth with us and they are also gifts from our Father.

There are the Jewish people that are still living today that are practicing their faith. I pray to God their eyes will be opened, that they will open the door to Jesus and to His Mother Mary so that He can heal their mind body soul and spirit, through the Holy Spirit and the exercise of God's Almighty Power and Jesus Christ Crucified. I also pray for all Christian faiths that haven't experienced our Lords Almighty Power in Jesus Christ Crucified, that they will find true salvation. I pray that all my brothers and sisters in Christ will find their way home and that they will also get to experience Everlasting Life in the new heaven and new earth today. I ask Almighty Father through Jesus Christ His Son and with Holy Mother Mary and all the Angels, Saints and Martyrs that have done your will throughout time and space to please open their eyes, so they can choose to bless you and bless themselves and everyone around them through a conversion of mind body soul and spirit and this conversion would also lead your people to Mary's Immaculate Heart. Our Father who art in Heaven: can do this and will, when we show that we are freely willing and choosing to cooperate with His Divine Will. Our prayers have been heard and we are to go on living and loving and trusting in God, that the whole world is in His hands. We are concerned with having the eye's accommodated, that God's children will see perfectly, especially if they cannot hear our Father calling them home. In regard to Gods children and His Kingdom, God is all knowing and all loving. And He shares all things with us. We are still growing with and in His love and in His knowledge and we can move forward on a straight and narrow path.

Through faith and grace and at His coming we are given sight, our vision has different decrees of light; we will be given only what we are capable of accepting and believing. So in this way we as a whole will possess Christ and we will be moving forward and growing in the Beatific Vision towards our goal which is Heaven on Earth. It can be done and it has been done and it will be done from one generation to the next. And when our life comes to an end and we fall asleep we know that Jesus Christ is with us and He will be their waiting to wake us from our sleep. And in this way we are able to stay in a state of grace that is pleasing to God Almighty.

Chapter 7

July 22, 2010 Feast of Mary Magdalene

What an awesome day to celebrate the risen Lord, with Mary Magdalene. How Jesus revealed Himself to her. What joy, we know that the people that lived before us that have been canonized Saints are dwelling in heaven. This is why I added them to my Book. Because: I also see them in the New Heaven and New Earth. Then I added pictures of my friends and family that I see here. I have noticed that they look a lot alike and some of them even have the same first names or last and even some have both first and last names alike. Some people would say just a coincidence; some people would say they don't look alike at all. And some people would say how dare you!

But because I see them in heaven on earth, the Saints living and loving and never dying, and always living to intercede for those of us, (the unbelievers and sinners that are living or dead). I am most grateful. But because of the signs and the times, I am being drawn by God to the spiritual world. And in the spiritual world in the new heaven and new earth, this is where heaven and earth meet. This leaves me open to experience all things, so I find myself trying to make sense of it all. So I know I must not be of the earthly world there I will reap death. So when I find myself in the realm of spirit and truth I seek for answers. I know both dimensions contain living, but only the earthly world contains sin and death. And so when the two dimensions heaven and earth become one under God, sin and death has been destroyed by Jesus Christ Crucified with God's Almighty Power, I am left with perpetual life, living and loving and never dying, always there interceding for the living and the dead with and in Jesus Christ and all those that dwell with and in Him also. And this is a major privilege.

So we have discussed the worldly and the Spiritual explanations, now we can move to the logical explanation. I believe I can explain it logically also. We know that we exist from one generation to the next through our ancestors and our descendants. And in each generation we are to be regenerated. So in this conversion of mind body soul and spirit, we can experience our true blood line. And we can trace it back to some degree. I don't know if there is any one that can go back two thousand years or more, to be able to prove their blood line. But one thing for sure we know we are of old blood. So drawing from old blood I can honestly say that it is possible that the people I see that look like the Saints are perhaps their descendants, and how beautiful they are, and because of the signs and times of God how much they truly look alike. Due to all these reasons I felt it important and honorable to include in my book what I see, so I could share my joy.

When we find ourselves in this state of grace, we can greet each other as if we have known each other for a long time, we are not strangers, give them a big hug and tell them its really nice to see you again. "When you meet people in the new heaven and new earth you can treat them like you already know them and love them." (God the Father manifested in Ron Miller spoke this to me). To some of us, these things might scare us. But the truth is do not be afraid, do not live in fear, it will only hold you back. The only healthy fear I know is the fear of God.

We are moving forward not backwards and are we willing and able to take a leap of faith? Rejoice and live and enjoy each other and everything God has given us. Be grateful children, when we show our gratitude we are able to say not I Lord, but you. You are all things to me, without you I am nothing I cease to be. So in this reality that we dwell, we can see and hear and feel God Almighty shaking the world, all the bad is falling and only the good remains.

I can see that the blood line of Jesus Christ and His relatives are still living today and that the door to adoption is still open and remains open for all eternity. This knowledge that God bestows upon His children is most precious to Him and us. And it should make us fall down in adoration before Him in tears of joy. And all of this can be shared with each other, so that it can be given to our Father with love and concern for all involved. And in this way we are all one with and in Jesus Christ his body. Do you think Almighty Father is proud of His children when we behave in this way? I believe so, and I look forward to the day when we all can bring to Almighty Father the love and concern due Him, through Jesus Christ Crucified, in the Unity of the Holy Spirit in God's Almighty Power.

All our work is offered through the Holy Spirit up to Almighty God through Jesus Christ Crucified in and through our dear sweet Mother Mary's hands and if we have sinned or offended thee in any way, or taken from your most Holy Word or added too, then may I be judged accordingly. But if our work has pleased you, may your blessing be upon us, and upon everyone that has helped us to make this the best it could possibly be, Thank you dear kind and loving Father for your Son and our Mother, all my family and friends and all your children where ever they may be. I realize without the Trinity I would not want to be. I ask you to please never stop loving and to always be merciful, and then I remember you never change and this I can count on, so all my worries are gone. We have been given everlasting life with and in Jesus Christ, to live with and in His love, and we live through Him, with Him and in Him. Jesus Christ lives forever, we the members of His Holy body also live forever, and we have become one with and in Him always living to intercede. And it makes us very happy to do so, just ask us.

"Father, the body of your risen Son is the temple not made by human hands and the defending wall of the New Jerusalem. May this holy city, built of living stones, shine with spiritual radiance and witness to your greatness in the sight of all nations." (Divine Office page 752).

"Thus says the Lord: The heavens are my throne, and the earth is my footstool. What kind of house can you build for me; what is to be my resting place? My hand made all these things when all of them came to be, says the Lord. This is the one whom I approve: the lowly and afflicted man who trembles at me word." (Divine Office page 752 Isaiah 66:1-2).

Thank You Father: for our spiritual death and our physical death that we might share in your Sons resurrection through the Holy Spirit with your Almighty Power in Jesus Christ Crucified. We can be at peace; we can live with and in your love, knowing that we shall never die. And when our life as we know it comes to and end and we experience spiritual death and or physical death we know whether living or dead we are united in Jesus Christ, our faith can tell us that we are in heaven on earth. Only when Jesus Christ comes and resurrects us from spiritual death and or physical death are we restored to our principle of life and we the living and the dead realize that we like our Mother Mary live perpetually in heaven on earth with all God's family that it can be all one, this is the life that our Father has promised to give all His children living or dead when He returns in His glory. Hallelujah, Hallelujah, Hallelujah.

We love knowing that we are part of the Trinity, thank you Father, Son and Holy Spirit for giving us life with and in Thee, thank you for our many blessings. Thank You: Trinity, for being The Men that you are and for giving us everlasting life, and the ability to live with Thee and in Thee in heaven on earth. Thank you for giving us the privilege of knowing you and loving you. We salute you in the name of the Father, Son and Holy Spirit. We do believe and we are very grateful for all things the good and the bad in our lives, because you heavenly Father can draw good from the bad, and make things new, so that we can better serve you. We find ourselves most content in what you have given us, so please except our grateful hearts; with all our love we salute you again.

Thank you Father for being faithful and truth to your word. Thank you for sending your Holy Spirit into our world and for sending your Son to redeem your people. We are at peace, and we are living with and in your love. And this love that we posses is the Trinity. "I am so in love with the Trinity manifested in my husband Billy, my true love. I look forward to living with Thee, in Thee and living in your love for all eternity." May our boundaries grow and your lands continue to expand in time and space in Jesus' name, Amen.

Sept. 14, 2010 the feast of the Exaltation of the Holy Cross

It is only with and in Jesus and through what God has given to me that I am able to share with you through the Holy Spirit. With much respect I come boldly and freely with death, life and truth with Jesus Christ Himself, for all, through the exercise of God's Almighty Power and Jesus Christ Crucified through the Holy Spirit. I am handing to your head good works for the treasury which bring death, life and truth with Jesus Christ Himself. And in this heavenly and earthly existence we are experiencing what God our Father wants for all His children. That we might grow to know Him and love Him, and to be with and in Him for all eternity. For all His children to unite as one in His Holy body in the unity of His Holy Spirit through the Spirit of Truth, forever more. Always and ever remember Our Father is Spirit and Truth. Amen. Amen. Glory, glory halleluiah, glory, glory halleluiah, glory, glory halleluiah His truth goes marching on.

From where I sit with and in God, which is heaven on earth. I see that God has and will raise the dead that we have and will be born again, that we have and will be reborn into God's kingdom. That God has been faithful and true to His Word. I believe when we conceive the Holy Spirit without sin we have a conversion of mind, body, soul and spirit which produces in us a pure heart, and everlasting life in heaven on earth. And I also believe when Jesus Christ returns in the Second Coming, the kingdom of God becomes a present reality through a vision and a dream substantiated through a glorious manifestation of Christ himself as a man, which for me and hopefully you the hearer is Billy Easley my husband. And all this activity is happening with and in the Holy Spirit through God's Almighty Power.

I am going to quote from the Holy Bible's Dictionary regarding the things I have written pertaining to the veil being lifted, my vision and dream and the manifestation that I testify to and what they mean, that you will also be able to verify what I have written to be true. It will also bring to light the oracles of the past, and the present, and hopefully the future: That the dynasty of the Jewish blood line is living and they are my family members. I believe my faith is based on Revelation itself with sound principles due to my surroundings and my resources. So in this way my faith and my present reality is a gift from God, I did nothing to deserve this love.

I would like the hearer to read about: MESSIAH, MESSIANISM it will enlighten you as to the past, present and future of God's Kingdom. "Messiah is the transcription of the Hebrew word Mashiah which means "anointed". In the New Testament and in the post-biblical Jewish writings it designates the king, son of David, who will bring about the definitive salvation of his people at the end of time. It is however never used in this sense in the Old Testament. In the Old Testament "the anointed one", or 'the anointed of the Lord" means the king or any king, and it alludes to the rite of anointing with which the king was enthroned in his kingly dignity, in virtue of which he became a sacred and untouchable person. The historical books of the Old Testament explicitly mention the anointing of Saul (1 Sam. 19:1-3), David (1 Sam. 16:13), Solomon (1 Kings 1:39), Jehu (2 Kings 9:6-8), Jehoash (2 Kings 11:12) and Jehoahaz (2 Kings 23:30). The sacred character of the person of the king is well expressed by David, who though he had Saul in his power did not dare touch his person: "I will not raise a hand against my Lord, for he is the Lord's anointed and a father to me: (1 Sam. 24:11). For the same reason David punished with death Saul's servant who at Saul's wish had killed him on the mountains of Gelboe:

"You are responsible for your own death, for you testified against yourself when you said, "I dispatched the Lord's anointed' " (2 Sam. 1:16).

Messianism is the hope of a future salvation to be accomplished by an anointed king of the family of David. We pass over the other soteriological figures of the Old Testament that do not have this explicit regal and Davidic character, such as the Servant of Yahweh and the Son of Man (see SERVANT OF THE LORD, SON OF MAN). In defining messianism we have spoken of the future to embrace the diverse forms that the messianic hope took down through the history of Israel. The term eschatological will be reserved to what appertains to the end of time, when history reaches its terminus. Eschatology supposes a universal point of view that takes up the question of the history of all peoples. It is a common opinion that such eschatology is only present in the Bible after the exile and develops its most decisive forms only with the apocalyptic writings. Messianism is certainly eschatological at this time, but to begin to distinguish messianism and eschatology would involve us in profitless difficulties when the point of the examination is messianism at its birth and first development. It is certain that the messianic hope, such as we find it in the New Testament writings, did not come about all at once at a certain moment in time. It underwent transformations and adjustments in the light of the course of salvation history itself. When the most ancient messianic oracles of the Old Testament are subjected to analysis in the light of the New Testament, the difficulty arises of how to determine the sense in which these speak of Christ. This poses the dilemma: either chooses a direct, literal messianic interpretation, or a typical one. In the first case, the text would speak directly of the future eschatological messiah. The second however seems to be eluding the problem, that is, account is taken of the fact that the New Testament quotes the texts of the Old Testament and applies them to Christ, but the exegete finds himself in difficulties. On the other hand the direct literal interpretation seems to have to ignore the historical situation in which these oracles were pronounced and their only too clear reference to a historical king.

Perhaps this difficulty can find a solution in the development of the messianic hope itself. The messianic hope has its ultimate roots in the soteriological function played by the king in the eyes of the ancient peoples of the East. What shines out in the king is not his majesty, dignity and power. These qualities follow on and are justified in the fact that the king is the person who guarantees the well-being and social harmony of the people by just and equitable government. (see JUSTICE) It is the king who leads the people to victory in battle, saves it from what might injure it, and takes immediate care of it for the benefit of his subjects. When the people ask Samuel for a king, what they really want is a savior. There must be a king over us. We too must be like other nations, with a king to rule us and to lead us in warfare and fight our battles". What does 'to rule us' mean in practice? This is expressed in concrete terms in Psalm 72:1-4: "O God, with your judgment endow the king . . . he shall govern your people with justice and your afflicted ones with judgment, the mountains shall yield place for the people, and the hills justice. He shall defend the afflicted among the people, save the children of the poor, and crush the oppressor this text is moreover interesting because all authors consider it to be messianic. The messianic hope then, at first reading, appears to be nourished by what people expected of a king, but to these expectations is added a divine pledge and guarantee.

This divine pledge to make promise a reality is contained in the oracle transmitted by Nathan to David (2 Sam. 7; 1 Chron. 17). David had shortly before that transferred the Ark of the Covenant to Jerusalem, and had decided to build for the Lord a house (Heb. Bayth). Nathan communicates to David an oracle on the point. In the first part he dissuades David from his project. "Should you build me a house to dwell in?" (2 Sam. 7:5). But he goes on: "The Lord also reveals to you that he will establish a house (bayth) for you" (2 Sam. 7:11). In this second part the word 'house' is not used in the sense of building, but in the sense of descent or lineage, of continuity in the family and therefore of dynasty. It is not a question of a strict biological continuity, but of a dynasty in which the hopes that surround every kingly figure will be kept alive and made into a reality (2 Sam. 7:14-16). The first part of God's discourse might seem to be a reproof, but in reality God accepts and is pleased with what Psalm 132 calls David's "anxious care" for the Ark of the Lord (Ps. 132:1-10). In this psalm too Nathan's oracle in favor of David is an answer by God to his piety (Ps. 132:11-13). God then freely pledges himself with an oath, a promise (Ps. 132:11) and a covenant (2 Sam. 23:5) to David and his dynasty: "Your house and your kingdom shall endure forever before me; your throne shall stand firm forever: (2 Sam. 7:16). This pledge is given by God not only in favor of David, but above all in favor of the people to whom David is king. God chooses David and his dynasty to bring into effect his designs for the salvation of Israel. "I will make you famous like the great ones of the earth. I will fix a place for my people Israel. I will plant them so that they may dwell in their place without further disturbance" (2 Sam. 7:10, 11). In a certain sense it could be said that the saving designs of Sinai were concentrated in the person of the king, whom God wished to associate with his saving will for Israel in the future. Just as the Covenant of Sinai demanded reciprocation, so also did the promise to the king. His personal conduct and attitude can not only condition the response of the people, but he can also draw on himself and his people the curses that the covenant itself held over the heads of transgressors. He could then put obstacles in the way of the immediate realization of God's plan of salvation, but not even his sins would force God to revoke the pledge he had taken towards David's monarchy; "If his (David's) sons forsake my law . . . I will punish their crime with a rod and their guilt with stripes. Yet my kindness I will not take from him, nor will I belie by faithfulness: (Ps. 89:33-34). Through Nathan's oracle then, God chose David and his successors forever as the instrument for the realization of his design for salvation. The messianic hope is as open to the future as is God's plan itself. As history unfolded, the vague outline of this plan became less and less vague. We will briefly outline this development in the consciousness of Israel throughout its history.

It is obvious that the messianic promise had a message of good news and hope for each individual king. Before it looked to the distant future, messianism integrated the institution of the monarchy in the institution of the Covenant. The initial antagonism between the two, that God through Samuel's mouth indicated to the Jews who were demanding a king, was overcome: "It is not you they reject, they are rejecting me as their king: (1 Sam 8:7; see KING), God himself put his seal on the monarchy as the means through which he would bring about salvation. The promise made to David finds its resonance in the hymns that accompany the enthronement of every king (Pss. 2 and 110; see also Ps. 72). In their immediate and more ancient sense, these were enthronement hymns (see 1 Kings l: 32:48; 2 Kings 11:12-20). The king was enthroned in the Temple. The priest consigned to him the insignia of his office, the diadem and a document called the "Solemn Statute" or "Pact", whose content, as is evidenced in Psalm 89:40, was nothing other than the promise of which 2 Sam. 7 speaks. This was a writing in which to the king was given divine affiliation in the sense that this has in the Old Testament (see SON OF GOD), together with the promise of divine assistance in what Ps. 2:7 calls the "decree of the king"; "I will proclaim the decree of the Lord: the Lord said to me: You are my son; this day I have begotten you. Ask of me and I will give you the nations for an inheritance, etc." Psalm 110 puts it more poetically: "Rule in the midst of your enemies. Yours is princely power in the day of your birth, in holy splendor; before the day star like the dew I have begotten you" (Ps. 110:2, 3). Then he is given the scepter (Ps. 110:2). After the anointing the king is acclaimed (1 Sam. 10:24; 2 Sam. 16:16; 2 Kings 9:13). Then he proceeds from the Temple to the place where, seated on his throne, he received the homage of his subjects (Ps. 110:1: 1 Kings 1:46). Psalms 2 and 110 are messianic because they give expression to the oracle of Nathan in 2 Sam. 7 and proclaim it for every king.

While it was applied to every king however, the messianic promise itself remained open to the future, just as did the plan of salvation for Israel. The history of salvation did not just have a past, from the patriarchs to the entry into the land of Canaan (see Deut. 26:5-10; Ps. 136). The history of salvation was future-directed. The Jews experienced a real tension between the glorious promises of the past and their but limited realization in the present. So they awaited an intervention by God in the future, the "Day of the Lord" in which would be fully realized all that was promised. This hope in a certain sense was already eschatological, for it was to be the decisive and concluding act the drama started with the promise. On the other hand however it was not fully eschatological because it is not seen in the context of a universal plan of God embracing all peoples and all history.

The messianic hope is caught up in an opening to the future. The promises made to David are made concrete in the king of the future who will be God's instrument in the realizations of salvation. This will be the new David, not just because he will be David's son, but because in him will return the piety, justice and power that David enjoyed. The ideal will have been achieved. The chief singer of this king is Isaiah.

The circumstances in which Isaiah exercised his ministry are well known (Is. 7). The continuity of the house of David was now in danger. Rezin of Damascus and Pekah of Israel have invaded Judah and have threatened to depose Ahaz if the latter does not fight with them against Tiglathpileser of Assyria. Isaiah exhorts the king to faith and calm, for his enemies will not see success. Despite the refusal of Ahaz to ask for a sign as warranty of the truth of the oracle, Isaiah offers one, that of Emmanuel. "The virgin shall be with child and bear a son, and shall name him Immanuel. . . . Before the child learns to reject the bad and choose the good, the land of those two kings who you (Ahaz) dread shall be deserted" (Is. 7:14-16). In the article on Emmanuel we have pointed out the reasons why Isaiah was directly referring to the future king Hezekiah. (see EMMANUEL) The two messianic oracles of 9:1-6 and 11:1-9 seem also to have been applied to king Hezekiah, and refer in all probability to his birth. The personage described by Isaiah however is not in the same line or on the same level as the kings hitherto, even the holy ones among them. Before the prophetic eyes arises a perfect and ideal figure, not just a model to imitate or a program to follow (see v.gr. Ps. 101) but a person whose reality is postulated and therefore guaranteed by the promise made to David.

It is true that Isaiah sees him already born in Hezekiah, but what is important and what was well understood by those who gathered his oracles is the taking shape, on the horizons of the future of messianic promise, the reality of a savior, son of David, who will bring to fruition the hopes that had hitherto eluded the empirical monarchy. Did Isaiah err then when he thought of Hezekiah? When the question is asked like this it does not make sense. Isaiah had his own tragic part to play like every precursor, just as had John the Baptizer, when through his disciples he asked

Jesus: "Are you 'He who is to come' or do we look for another?" (Matt. 11:3). There could be confusion in the identification of those signs which are meant to reveal the event of which they are

Heralds, Isaiah did not apply to Hezekiah the ideal image of the messianic king which was well known and awaited. Rather the political turn of events and other circumstances that preceded and accompanied the birth of the king opened the eyes of the prophet to the meaning of the messianic promise to be realized in a perfect and ideal king.

From then on the empirical monarchy, that is, the effective succession of kings remained in a sense outside the messianic promise, except as a link with the future king, who was to be son of David. However this was a prelude, an antecedent condition for the realization of the promise. This is why there was profound disturbance when the dynastic continuity was irreparably interrupted by the exile. One can notice an echo of this tragic sense in Ps. 89:39-52: it seemed to make void the whole promise. Even this however was overcome in the prospects opened up by the prophets who foresee the restoration of the kingdom at the end of the exile. Then the Messiah, the new David, will take his place at the head of his people (Jer. 23:5, 6; Ezek. 34:23; 37; 24). Zerubbabel, the head of the Jewish community that returned from exile in Babylonia becomes the center on whom converge the messianic hopes (Hag. 2:20; Zech. 6:9). Deutero-Isaiah purifies the image of the king-Savior from the excessive external splendor so often associated with him, and presents him as a ""just savior, meek and riding on an ass, on a colt, the foal of an ass" (Zech. 9:9-13).

In the Jewish literature between the two testaments an intense messianic fervor is noticeable. Here a few points should be underlined. The more popular messianism, nurtured under the harsh experience of the Roman oppression, aspired to the overthrow of this dominion and so it automatically took on a political color with all its intolerance for the oppressor. This sparked the revolt of the Zealots. (see ZEALOTS) There were not a few false messiahs in New Testament times (see Acts 5:35-39). Messianic movements were then naturally held in suspicion buy the Romans. With this messianic idea as a foundation, a great variety of eschatological speculation was carried on, with computations and minute descriptions of the different phases of the last times, in the center of which appeared the different figures of a savior, who often gathered into himself elements from different traditions.: he was to be a Davidic messiah and the Son of Man. The Targum identifies the Servant of Yahweh of Is. 41:1 with the messiah, while the apocryphal work, the Fourth Book of Esdras and the Apocalypse of Baruch adorn the Davidic messiah with elements taken from the Son of Man.

On the messianic consciousness of Jesus see JESUS CHRIST, MESSIANIC SECRET, Here must suffice a few words on the interpretation given to some of the messianic texts by the New Testament. First of all it must be kept in mind that the point of departure in reading the New Testament is the reality of Christ, who clarifies the meaning of Scripture. This was no novelty. It was the final unfolding of the meaning of the oracles and promises as they were seen through the developing history of Israel. The oracle of Nathan remained open to the future just as much as did the salvific plan of God of which it was a promise and apart. What was a thumb-nail sketch in Nathan was filled in through the action of God in history. The oracles of Isaiah were a rereading of 2 Sam. 7. Ezek. 21:32 took up the blessing of Jacob on Judah (Gen. 49:10). While the Greek version of the Bible, the Septuagint, discovered in the Proto-evangelium itself, Gen. 3:15 the figure of the Messiah (see PROTOEVANGELIUM). With the resurrection of Christ however the vague lines were clarified and brought to convergence, and the messianic oracles were seen in their most profound significance. Pss. 2:7 and 110 which are often quoted in the New Testament are gradually interpreted as applying to the eternal generation of the Word. The "Today" of Ps. 2:7 becomes the crowning moment of Christ's mission, when, arisen from the dead, as man he takes possession of his rightful glory at the right hand of God in the heavens: (Heb. 1:5 5:5; 6:20; Acts 13:34 Rom. 1:4). When Psalm 110:1 is linked up with Dan. 7:13, it refers to the same moment: Christ's enthronement at the right hand of God. Christ's resurrection and exaltation to the right hand of God is the solemn enthronement of the Messiah king of whom the Psalm sang. But all is not yet brought to completion. 1 Cor. 15:27 and Heb. 10:13 still await the perfect fulfillment of Ps. 110:1, 2. What the Old Testament says of the messianic kingdom is unfolding to its full flowering in the time between Christ's own exaltation and his second coming. This is the era of the Church. Already in the flesh of Christ have the messianic oracles found their fulfillment, but they still await their full and perfect realization when the kingdom of Christ and God will be manifested in all its fullness". (Holy Bible NAB). "MESSIANIC SECRET, "The Messianic Secret in the Gospels" is the celebrated title of a study by W. Wrede, who for the first time subjected to systematic study a rather surprising aspect of Jesus" preaching in regard to his messiahship. This surprising aspect is that, especially according to Mark, Jesus goes to great pains to hide his messiahship. For this reason he imposes silence on the demoniacs who recognize him (Mark 1:22-25; 3:3-5), while he obliges the cured to silence about their miracle (Mark 1:40-45; 5:21-43; 7:31-37; 8:22-26). Later he imposes silence on Peter, when, in the name of all, he confesses Jesus" messiahship (Mark 8:30). Wrede's explanation for this was the following: the messianic secret was Mark's own invention. His intention was to reconcile the faith of the Church of his time, which proclaimed Jesus Messiah, with the more ancient tradition on Jesus and with the historical reality, in which nothing had been said about the messiahship of Jesus. Instead of changing the ancient tradition to meet the faith of the Church of his day, Mark explained the silence by attributing to Jesus the clear intention of keeping his messiahship hidden until it should be revealed with his resurrection. Although Wrede's theory is ingenious and arbitrary, it had the merit of focusing attention of this real problem, on which up to this no fully satisfying solution has been established. If it is true that the messianic secret is put into particular relief by Mark, it is equally true that Mark is not its inventor. In fact the secret mirrors a historical attitude of Jesus. It is also planted as a thesis at the beginning of the discourse in parable, when Jesus turned to his disciples and said: "To you the mystery of the reign of God has been confided. To the others outside it is all presented in parables: (Mark 4:11). The parables are not self evident explanations of the mystery of the kingdom of God for the non-initiated. Several of them more than need an explanation. They are rather the vehicles of a revelation in mystery, in veiled allusion, demanding an explanation that Jesus reserves for the few. This procedure has a parallel in the apocalyptic tradition, and precisely in regard to the Son of Man. (see SON OF MAN) In fact, according to this tradition, the Son of Man already exists and is hidden with God. His glorious manifestation will take place at the end of time. Before this comes, however, his existence and the other eschatological mysteries have been revealed to a chosen few, that is, to those who by special privilege have been admitted for a time behind the veil to receive the vision. These privileged people are the ancient personages to whom the apocalyptic books have falsely been attributed. These in turn reveal what they have seen to a select group of pious and just men, who then are encouraged and established in their hopes by this revelation. In the same way Jesus enveloped in mystery his self- revelation and that of the mysteries of the kingdom of God, which, in the final analysis are one and the same thing. In him and through him the kingdom of God, which, in the final analysis are one and the same thing. In him and through him the kingdom of God becomes a present reality. What is the intention and scope of this conduct of Jesus? Different explanations have been offered, which do not exclude one another but are rather complementary, and move at different levels of profoundity. From the first centuries of the Christian era, the silence that Jesus imposed was explained as a measure of prudence so that his mission might not be compromised by an equivocation that could prove fatal. Popular messianism had taken on a political and seditious character, so that the mere name of Messiah was enough to move the people to an erroneous enthusiasm about the real mission of Jesus, and at the same time provoke the suspicions of the constituted authority in the land.

As time went on however, it was not just a measure of prudence, seeing the deformation that the concept of Messiah had undergone. The secret was an indispensable condition for faith in him. By means of the secret Jesus showed his reluctance to allow himself to be framed and, as it were, trapped within the confines of an already shaped title. It was possible to give to Jesus openly the title of Messiah without these equivocations and without these dangers to the faith, when the title itself was no longer a box into which to close Jesus, but the reality of Jesus himself dictated to the title its contents. Messiahship means continuity with the promise, that is, with the whole history of salvation. The idea of messiah however that had formed during the times of promise was inadequate to the reality of Christ: in the light of his coming the promises could really be understood. This is why the Old Testament was avidly read in the light of its fulfillment in the New. The Old prophecies were searched for traces of the unexpected newness that was Christ. Since it was the reality of Christ that gave to the title Messiah its content, the messiahship itself finished up by being contained in the name of the savior, Jesus Christ.

In the final analysis however the messianic secret does not rest on the plane of Jesus' attitude. For this attitude signals something much more profound: the great and radical hiddenness of Christ is his incarnation that redeemed, an enfleshment totally similar to ours except that he made no concession to sin. While he was God, he came in the form of a slave by emptying himself (Phil. 2l5 ff.). The mystery of the enfleshed Word then could not become transparent in all its splendor accept when the risen and exalted Christ took possession also as man of his universal saving dominion, the fruit of his death. This is why he is called Christ without danger of ambiguity, a mystery he had hidden while he still walked in the form of a slave." (The Catholic Holy Bible: Bible dictionary and concordance Page 148). The definition of Apocalyptic is Revelation you can also look that up on page 10 in the Catholic Holy Bible nab,nve the location is in the dictionary and concordance. The Apocalyptic literature that has been written and also what I have wrote is what the Church teaches, and also what the Gospels preach. So now I hope and pray we are all on the same page of understanding. And perhaps the Church will embrace and acknowledge W. Wrede's writings and have all truth established, and substantiated we definitely are speaking about the same things. With substantiation it would give embodiment to our work. (The Second Coming of Jesus Christ through a lifting of the veil, a vision, dream and a glorious manifestation of Jesus Christ as a Man, which is revealed through Billy

Easley and a glorious manifestation of God the Father in Ron Miller reigning in heaven on earth).

"Lord, do not judge us according to our deeds: We have done nothing worthy in your sight, therefore we implore you, God of majesty, - blot out all our guilt. Lord, wash away our iniquities, and cleanse us from our sins". (Divine Office Page: 1482). Behold the fruit from Mary's womb, the Lamb of God who takes away the sins of the world. Happy are those who are called to His supper. Take and eat, that Jesus may heal your mind, body, soul and spirit. Open wide your mouth, be filled that all things may be fulfilled in you.

Pertaining to mine and hopefully your reality in the end Jesus did come, he lifted the veil of understanding through the Holy Spirit in a vision and a dream and also through a manifestation as a man in my husband Billy Easley, and also God the Father was revealed through the Holy Spirit manifested in Ron Miller. The Trinity was revealed to me, thus I share with the hearer. And the spirit that Jesus Christ sent to us was the spirit of fire and truth. That spirit is the Holy Spirit and it sets us free and on fire. Through Jesus Christ Crucified in God's Almighty Power we are made new through the Holy Spirit. We the unbelievers and sinners that were with Jesus at His Crucifixion with Mary experienced spiritual death through the exercise of God's Almighty Power. Everyone died by the sword and also died to sin and evil with much grief with and in Jesus Christ at the foot of the cross in Jerusalem, except for Mary she was born without sin. The lance that pierced her Son, also pierced Mary's' heart, thus creating a sorrowful moment for all but above all Mary, so that the thoughts of many hearts may be revealed. And she Mary did experience spiritual death also. Thus we experienced a spiritual death with Jesus Christ's physical death. The spirit of fire set our world, the dead on fire and we were purified. Through the Holy Spirit in God's Almighty Power we the unbelievers and the sinners were converted to the truth and brought to life with and in Jesus Christ thus experienced the first resurrection of the dead. We the redeemed members of Jesus' body were released from limbo and we were purified by fire in purgatory by the word of God. We were resurrected from the dead in Jerusalem with and in our Savior Jesus Christ through the Holy Spirit in God's Almighty Power, we went with and in Jesus to the location of the dead where those that were waiting to be resurrected from Adam and Eve till Jesus Christ could come and resurrect them. We with and in Jesus the members of His resurrected body went with our Savior Jesus Christ to the "underworld" when He ministered to all those stuck in limbo and purgatory, thus He set all of us free from our captivity, giving all of us life with Him and in Him in heaven on earth through the Holy Spirit in God's Almighty Power. We the hearer's experienced spiritual death we experienced limbo and also purgatory. We the members of Jesus body experienced the abode of the dead with and in Jesus our Savior. We experienced the first resurrection of the dead with and in Jesus, with all the souls from the beginning of time and space. Thus we ascended to heaven on earth with and in Jesus Christ Crucified through the Holy Spirit in God's Almighty Power. We are Jesus' sheep. We were brought to a new spiritual life with Him and in Him through the Holy Spirit in God's Almighty Power. And those in Jerusalem that were still living could see the dead coming out of the ground from their graves that had been dead, yet now living. And we with and in our Savior ascended to Jesus Christ's Throne: the new heaven and new earth. The old world passed away in the spirit, and we have become the New Israel. If we accept and believe our faith tells us that Jesus descended to the abode of the dead the underworld and He ministered to all the souls from the beginning of time to the end of time that had been held captive. So that when He ascends to heaven, all souls from all time and space could follow our Savior home, that we would be taken with Him and in Him, through the Holy Spirit in God's Almighty Power.

I believe we the redeemed from all time and space did, have and will by faith and grace and deeds done with and in Jesus Christ Crucified through the Holy Spirit in God's Almighty Power did, have and will ascend to the Throne with and in our Savior Jesus Christ. That the ones with the deeds done in Jesus Christ Crucified through the Holy Spirit in God's Almighty Power are of the first resurrection and we live forever by the gift of eternal life with and in our Savior Jesus Christ. That we are all truly blessed, and that Jesus is offering eternal life to all His children now and forever more. I believe in universalism, when all accept and all believe in Jesus Christ whether at spiritual death and or at physical, that all may be saved. I also believe that the people living in Jerusalem at the time of the first resurrection truly saw Jesus and those that were raised from the dead walking the streets, and that it brought repentance, conversion an the truth upon their mind, body, soul and spirit, thus they were saved also. And to this day and forever more we can still see Jesus and those that followed Him walking the streets of Heaven on earth. That Judgment is a chance to profess our faith, Amen. This mystery has been revealed to the hearer and me at this very moment. "All who are in their graves shall hear the voice of the Son of God; - those who have done deeds will go forth to the resurrection of life; those who have done evil will go forth to the resurrection of judgment. In an instant, in the twinkling of an eye, at the final trumpet blast, the dead shall rise." (John 5:28-29; 1 Corinthians 15:52). When Jesus comes He brings His Armey of Angels, Saints and Martyrs with and in Him.

And He is mighty in Word and in deed. He is King of Kings Faithful and True, He is the Alpha and the Omega, the first and the last, the beginning and the end. This is the "Holy Way." "If the dead are not raised, neither has Christ been raised, and if Christ has not been raised, your faith is vain." (1 Corinthians 15:16-17). Our mind, body, soul and spirit are sown in weakness; our whole being is raised in Jesus Christ Crucified in God's Almighty Power through the Holy Spirit. Our body and the things they contain are sown in a natural body; thus raised up in a spiritual body. "Now that your obedience to charity has purified your souls for a brotherly love that is sincere, love one another heartily and intensely. For you have been reborn, not from corruptible seed but from incorruptible, through the word of God who lives and abides forever." (1 Peter. 1 22-25). My prayer is that the hearer through the Holy Spirit would also become the doer and gain merit thus reward for good deeds done with and in Jesus Christ Crucified in God's Almighty Power unto the Paschal Mystery. That faith, charity, hope, and love render the whole mystery of Christ that no one is left 4 dead, in Jesus name, Amen. The thought of those poor souls that are left behind, grief's me so. "The definition of Paschal Mystery is the title of a document, Paschalis Mysterii, issued by Pope Paul V1 on May 9, 1969. In this document he approved a reorganization of the liturgical year and calendar for the Roman Rite. Its purpose was "to permit the faithful to communicate in a more intense way, through faith, hope and love, in the whole mystery of Christ, which . . . unfolds within the cycle of a year." Paschal Mystery is a general term to describe the redemptive work of Christ, especially the events of the Last Supper and the Passion, reaching their climax on Easter Sunday, (Etym. Latin paschalis, from apscha, Passover, Easter; from Greek pascha; from Hebrew pesah, Pesach." (Modern Catholic Dictionary, John A. Hardon, S.J.).

Jesus Christ and our Almighty Father through the Holy Spirit are working miracles* I pray that we can keep up with our many blessings with and in Jesus Christ in our mind, body, soul and spirit.

"Truly with you God is hidden,* the God of Israel, the savior! Those are put to shame and disgrace* who vent their anger against him. Those go in disgrace who carve images. Israel, you are saved by the Lord, saved forever! You shall never be put to shame or disgrace in future ages.

For thus says the Lord, the creator of the heavens, who is God, the designer and maker of the earth who established it, not creating it to be a waste, but designing it to be lived in: I am the Lord, and there is no other. I have not spoken from hiding nor from some dark place of the earth. And I have not said to the descendants of Jacob, "Look for me in an empty waste." I, the Lord, promise justice, I foretell what is right.

Come and assemble, gather together, you fugitives from among the Gentiles! They are without knowledge who bear wooden idols and pray to gods that cannot save.

Come here and declare in counsel together: Who announced this from the beginning and foretold it from of old? Was it not I, the Lord, besides whom there is no other God? There is no just and saving God but me.

Turn to me and be safe, all you ends of the earth, for I am God; there is no other! By myself I swear, uttering my just decree and my unalterable word: To me every knee shall bend; by me every tongue shall swear, saying, "Only in the Lord are just deeds and power." Before him in shame shall come all who vent their anger against him. In the Lord shall be the vindication and the glory of all the descendants of Israel." (Isaiah 45:15-25).

"We praise you, the Lord God Almighty, who is and who was. You have assumed your great power; you have begun your reign. The nations have raged in anger, but your wrath has come, and the moment to judge the dead; the time to reward your servants the prophets and the holy ones who revere you, the great and the small alike.

Now have salvation and power come, the reign of our God and the authority of his Anointed One. For the accuser of our brothers is cast out, who night and day accused them before God. They defeated him by the blood of the Lamb and by the word of their testimony; love for life did not deter them from death. So rejoice you heavens, and you that dwell there in!" (Revelation 11:17-18; 12:10b-12a).

Spiritual death and physical death are elements in Creation and Spiritual Creation; if they are not there we do not have eternal life. The path is shown to you through my scroll as to where it starts and where it goes. This is not reincarnation; we that live in the spirit never eternally die and we live forever in heaven on earth, through Him, with Him, in Him, in the unity of the Holy Spirit, all Glory and Honor are yours Almighty Father forever and ever. So perhaps now people might understand why I love being a Catholic, my Church contains everything that I am. The Trinity upholds the world that I live in, my mother Mary is my exemplar. The Queen of Heaven and the Trinity are my best friend's they help me unconditionally and our love is mutual. All Mary's children are my brothers and sisters and I love them unconditionally with all my heart. My surroundings and my resources are my support; I am the bride of Jesus Christ, and I am fed from the altar the body and blood of our Savior Jesus Christ through the Holy Spirit by Jesus Christ' saints in heaven on earth. This is my home, and I am inviting any one that is hungry or thirsty to come to the banquet of life being offered, that you might also be fed and given the water of life, that flows freely from Jesus Christ through the Holy Spirit. "*The Spirit and the bride say, "Come." Let the hearer say, "Come." Let the one who thirsts come forward, and the one who wants it receive the gift of life-giving water." (Revelation 22:17). "The grace of the Lord Jesus be with all." (Revelation 22:21).

CHRIST WILL CHANGE OUR LOWLY BODY:

"To this end Christ died and rose to life that he might be Lord both of the dead and of the living. But God is not God of the dead, but of the living. That is why the dead, now under the dominion of one who has risen to life, are no longer dead but alive. Therefore life has dominion over them and, just as Christ, having been raised from the dead, will never die again, so too they will live and never fear death again. When they have been thus raised from the dead and freed from decay, they shall never again see death, for they will share in Christ's resurrection just as he himself shared in their death.

This is why Christ descended into the underworld, with its imperishable prison-bar: to shatter the doors of bronze and break the bars of iron and, from decay, to raise our life to himself by giving us freedom in place of servitude.

But if this plan does not yet appear to be perfectly realized- for men still die and bodies still decay in death- this should not occasion any loss of faith. For, in receiving the first fruits, we have already received the pledge of all the blessings we have mentioned; with them we have reached the heights of heaven, and we have taken our place beside him who has raised us up with himself, as Paul says: In Christ God has raised us up with him, and has made us sit with him in the heavenly places.

And the fulfillment will be ours on the day predetermined by the Father, when we shall put off our childish ways and come to perfect manhood. For this is the decree of the Father of the ages: the gift, once given, is to be secure and no more to be rejected by a return to childish attitudes.

There is no need to recall that the Lord rose from the dead with a spiritual body, since Paul in speaking of our Bodies bears witness that they are sown as animal bodies and raised as spiritual bodies: that is, they are transformed in accordance with the glorious transfiguration of Christ who goes before us as our Leader.

If this transformation is a change into a spiritual body and one, furthermore, like the glorious body of Christ, then Christ rose with a spiritual body, a body that was sown in dishonor, but the very body that was transformed in glory.

Having brought this body to the Father as the first fruits of our nature, he will also bring the whole body to fulfillment. For he promised this when he said: I, when I am lifted up, will draw all men to myself." (Divine Office Pages: 1484, 1485 from a sermon by Saint Anastasius of Antioch, bishop (Oratio 5, de Resurrectione Christi, 6-7. 9: PG 89, 1338-1359, and 1361-1362).

"Oppose, Lord, those who oppose me; war upon those who make war upon me. Take up the shield and buckler; rise up in my defense. Brandish lance and battle-ax against my pursuers. Say to my heart, "I am your salvation." Let those who seek my life be put to shame and disgrace. Let those who plot evil against me be turned back and confounded. Make them like chaff before the wind, with the angel of the Lord driving them on. Make their way slippery and dark, with the angel of the Lord pursuing them. Without cause they set their snare for me; without cause they dug a pit for me. Let ruin overtake them unawares; let the snare they have set catch them; let them fall into the pit they have dug. Then I will rejoice in the Lord, exult in God's salvation. My very bones shall say, "O Lord, who is like you, who rescue the afflicted from the powerful, the afflicted and needy from the despoiler?"

Malicious witnesses come forward, accuse me of things I do not know. They repay me evil for good and I am all alone. *Yet I, when they were ill, put on sackcloth, afflicted myself with fasting, sobbed my prayers upon my bosom. I went about in grief as for my brother, bent in mourning as for my mother. Yet when I stumbled they gathered with glee, gathered against me like strangers. They slandered me without ceasing; without respect they mocked me, gnashed their teeth against me.

Lord, how long will you look on? Save me from roaring beasts, my precious life from lions! Then I will thank you in the great assembly, I will praise you before the mighty throng. Do not let lying foes smirk at me, my undeserved enemies wink knowingly. They speak no words of peace, but against the quiet in the land they fashion deceitful speech. They open wide their mouths against me. They say, "Aha! Good! Our eyes relish the sight! You see this, Lord; do not be silent; Lord, do not withdraw from me. Awake, be vigilant in my defense, in my cause, my God and my Lord. Defend me because you are just, Lord; my God, do not let them gloat over me. Do not let them say in their hearts, "Aha! Just what we wanted!" Do not let them say, "We have devoured that one!" Put to shame and confound all who relish my misfortune. Clothe with shame and disgrace those who lord it over me. But let those who favor my just cause shout for joy and be glad. May they ever say, "Exalted be the Lord who delights in the peace of his loyal servant." Then my tongue shall recount your justice; declare your praise, all the day long." (Psalm 35).

"I waited, waited for the LORD; who bent down and heard my cry, Drew me out of the pit of destruction, out of the mud of the swamp, Set my feet upon rock, steadied my steps, And put a new song* in my mouth, a hymn to our God. Many shall look on in awe and they shall trust in the Lord. Happy those whose trust is the LORD, who turn not to idolatry or to those who stray after falsehood. How numerous, O LORD, my God, you have made your wondrous deeds! And in your plans for us there is none to equal you. Should I wish to declare or tell them, too many are they to recount. Sacrifice and offering you do not want; but ears open to obedience you gave me. Holocausts and sin-offerings you do not require; so I said, "Here I am; your commands for me are written in the scroll. To do your will is my delight; my God, your law is in my heart!" I announced your deed to a great assemble; I did not restrain my lips; You, Lord, are my witness. Your deed I did not hide within my heart; your loyal deliverance I have proclaimed. I made no secret of your enduring kindness to a great assemble. LORD, do not withhold your compassion from me; may your enduring kindness ever preserve me. For all about me are evils beyond count; my sins so overcome me I cannot see. They are more than the hairs of me head; my courage fails me. LORD, graciously rescue me! Come quickly to help me, LORD! Put to shame and confound all who seek to take my life. Turn back in disgrace those who desire my ruin. Let those who say "Aha!" Know dismay and shame. But may all who seek you rejoice and be glad in you. May those who long for your help always say, "The LORD be glorified." Though I am afflicted and poor, the Lord keeps me in mind. You are my help and deliverer: my God, do not delay!" (Psalm 40).

"Bless the LORD, my soul; all my being, bless his holy name! Bless the LORD, my soul; do not forget all the gifts of God, Who pardons all your sins, heals all your ills, Delivers your life from the pit, surrounds you with love and compassion, Fills your days with good things; your youth is renewed like the eagle's.* The LORD does righteous deeds, brings justice to all the oppressed. His ways were revealed to Moses, mighty deeds to the people of Israel. Merciful and gracious is the LORD, slow to anger, abounding in kindness. God does not always rebuke, nurses no lasting anger, Has not dealt with us as our sins merit, nor requited us as our deeds deserve. As the heavens tower over the earth, so God's love towers over the faithful. As far as the east is from the west, so far have our sins been removed from us. As a father has compassion on his children, so the LORD has compassion on the faithful. For he knows how we are formed, remembers that we are dust. Our days are like the grass; like flowers of the field we blossom. The wind sweeps over us and we are gone; our place knows us no more. But the LORD'S kindness is forever, toward the faithful from age to age. He favors the children's children of those who keep his covenant, who take care to fulfill its precepts. The LORD"S throne is established in heaven; God's royal power rules over all. Bless the LORD, all you angels, mighty in strength and attentive, obedient to every command. Bless the LORD all you hosts, ministers who do God's will. Bless the LORD, all creatures, everywhere in God's domain. Bless the LORD, my soul." (Psalm 103).

"Standing by the cross of Jesus was Mary his mother."

John 19-25

Sept. 15, 2010 Feast of our Lady of Sorrow

It is a wonderful thing to experience the sorrow of our Mother Mary that it may become our sorrow also, but along with the sorrow we can also experience all the other Mysteries as well. Take the time and experience the Mysteries while we are still in Jerusalem, under the influence of the Holy Spirit.

In honor of all the saints, and those declared living in heaven by the Catholic Church, I a member of the church acknowledge and acclaim that the mind, body, soul and spirit of these men and women live on, through the Holy Spirit with and in Jesus Christ the living word of God, in the communion of saints, all in God's Almighty Power and Jesus Christ Crucified. This is the faith of the bride of Jesus Christ.

That we bear fruit from the sorrow of Mary' heart: That it might produce in us the fruit of Jesus' death. That we would be able enter into the Holy of Holies. In this Holy of Holies nothing defiled or unclean can enter, and this is why God in His Almighty Power has to cleanse us and deliver us from the evil that is in our members, that we might come to God cleansed by His Son Jesus Christ through the Holy Spirit. That Jesus Christ through his love of God and His obedience unto death and unto His Father's will would produce in Himself and us the merit to present us to His Father unblemished and ready to

take the seat next to Him in heaven, to serve Him and His kingdom with all diligence. That we would become His priestly people set apart for good works unto the Lord. Our Attitude of the things of God through the Holy Spirit working with and in us along side Jesus Christ in God's Almighty Power have become for us this day a true reality and the will of God. That we the hearer, would become the doer in Jesus name, through God's Almighty Power, Amen. Thus through our Mother Mary's love and sorrowful heart, we would also be given a sorrowful and Immaculate heart alongside hers, in Jesus' name. That Jesus' great sacrifice would come down to us from the tree of life and the tree of knowledge. That Jesus' love and His great act of charity would produce in us the fruit needed to live on with and in Him; in heaven on earth and that we would choose not to physically die in our sin, all of us through the Holy Spirit with and in Jesus Christ Crucified all just deeds done with and in God's Almighty Power. Through fasting we have been given the fruit from the tree of life and of knowledge, that we may soar upward in mind, body, soul and spirit with and in Jesus Christ' body through the Holy Spirit and the exercise of God's Almighty Power. The lost Ark of the Covenant has been found in the Garden of Eden it is most Sacred and most Holy it is overflowing with God's Almighty Power it brings death, life and truth, the graces flow from the tree through the root with and in the vine to us the branches, all the fruit comes from the sacred hearts of Jesus and Mary, all through the hands of the Mother of God. That through, with and in the garden God might show His unending love unto us through the Holy Spirit.

AMAZING GRACE / MY CHAINS ARE GONE

1. Amazing grace, how sweet the sound That saved a wretch like me. I once was lost but now am found, was blind but now I see. 2. 'Twas grace that taught my heart to fear and grace my fears relieved; how precious did that grace appear, the hour I first believed! (to chorus); MY CHAINS ARE GONE. I'VE BEEN SET FREE. MY GOD, MY SAVIOR HAS RANSOMED ME. AND LIKE A FLOOD HIS MERCY REIGNS, UNENDING LOVE, AMAZING GRACE. 3. The Lord has promised good to me, His word my hope secures; He will my shield and portion be, as long as life endures (to chorus). 4. The earth shall soon dissolve like snow. The sun forbear to shine. But God who called me here below, will be forever mine. Will be forever mine. You are forever mine.

Sept. 27, 2010 Feast of Saint Vincent De Paul

Hail Mary full of grace the Lord is with you, blessed art though amongst women and blessed is the fruit of your womb, Jesus. Holy Mary, mother of God pray for us sinners now and at the hour of our death, Amen. "Truly, you are blessed among women. For you have changed Eve's curse into a blessing; and Adam, who hitherto lay under a curse, has been blessed because of you. Truly, you are blessed among women. Through you the Father's blessing has shown forth on mankind, setting them free of their ancient curse. Truly, you are blessed among women, because through you your forebears have found salvation. For you were to give birth to the Savior who was to win them salvation

Truly, you are blessed among women, for without seed you have borne, as your fruit, him who bestows blessings on the whole world and redeems it from that curse that made it sprout thorns. Truly, you are blessed among women, because, though a women by nature, you will become, in reality, God's mother. If he whom you are to bear is truly God made flesh, then rightly do we call you God's mother. For you have truly given birth to God." (Little Office of the Blessed Virgin Mary Pages: 13 and 14). "The Virgin has given birth to the Savior: a flower has sprung from Jesse's stock and a star has risen from Jacob. O God, we praise you. You are all beautiful, O Mary; in you there is no trace of original sin." (Little Office of the Blessed Virgin Mary Page: 14).

"I bud forth delights like the vine; my blossoms become fruit fair and rich. Come to me, all you that yearn for me, and be filled with my fruits; You will remember me as sweeter than honey, better to have than the honeycomb He who eats of me will hunger still, he who drinks of me will thirst for more; He who obeys me will not be put to shame, he who serves me will never fail." (Little Office of the Blessed Virgin Mary: Page 18). Oh Mary conceived without sin pray for us who have recourse to thee. We are invoking our Mother Mary and the Intercession from Saint Vincent De Paul that their prayers and ours would be pleasing to Our Father. That Mary would hand our prayers for the world, unto you sweet Jesus, that you may lay our hopes and our desires for the total good at the feet of God for us your children. Thank You Saint Vincent De Paul for all your hard work, that it would draw us your children closer to the Trinity. And thank you dear sweet heavenly Mother for being patient with us and always being there for us, that you might show us your Son, on earth. Thank you for holding God's arm back that we would not have to experience judgment. Rather we would be given time to repent and convert and experience Jesus' Divine Mercy. That our mind, body, soul and spirit through our spiritual lives would be levitated with elation like that of Saint Francis of Assisi'. That we could and would walk the clean streets of heaven and breathe the pure air of heaven and know that we have made it home safely. God's potential is the main source and we access it through the Holy Spirit with and in Jesus Christ Crucified in God's Almighty Power that we could and would become fruitful with and in the Trinity. As for the unbelievers and sinners in the beginning of secret sins I was counted among them. I with my brothers and sisters of the earth could and would ask Jesus and Mary into our hearts to stay. That all of us could and would grow and become more like Jesus and Mary, that we could and would pass through the gates of heaven together. That we could and would grow up together through the garden with and in Trinity, through the Holy Spirit in God's Almighty Power. Thus we could and would all learn to appreciate God and His Universe, I was hoping and praying for the Total Good of all.

Everyone entering heaven does so by the grace of God, through faith in Jesus Christ in God's Almighty Power. "In the Garden" In the beginning Adam and Eve were the examples for us pertaining to the tree of life and of knowledge. Their disobedience brought sin and death. We their children have learned from Adam and Eve and Jesus and Mary through the Holy Spirit in God's Almighty Power, that if we obey God and do what's right, just and lawful, that we could and would live forever with and in Jesus, and with the ones we love. Good and Evil are the examples of the tree of knowledge, by eating the good fruit from the tree of knowledge we gain truth. And by eating from the tree of life we gain eternal life.

Our path from and to the garden has been established in Genesis to Revelation. And we call this the Word of God. We go from and to the garden the "Holy Way." In this garden of life and knowledge that God planted in the beginning has today in the end, become Genesis through Revelations. As we sow and reap in the garden, God waters the garden and we become what are known to us. Thus we become known as we are known. The fruit from the trees of life and knowledge, and from the watering in the garden by God and the sowing and reaping God, Jesus, Joseph and Mary and all those in heaven become known to us.

And unto this end Jesus, Joseph, Mary and our Father and all those living with and in Jesus become our present reality here in the new heaven and new earth. The old world has passed away in the spirit and the new heavens and the new earth has come down from God Almighty through the Holy Spirit with and in Jesus Christ in us. The Old Israel has become the New Israel. That we may spend eternity with the ones we truly love. God plants the seed the tree grows Mary is the root of all things and through the root we are given Jesus through Mary's womb. Ignorance is no longer Bliss, but knowledge of eternal life with and in Jesus becomes our present reality and our bliss. In the beginning the root of evil produced poisonous fruit, by Eve. Through the New Covenant Mary being the root of the tree in the Garden of Eden naturally produced good fruit. (Jesus) From our own desire and free will we would want to draw from Mary's root, we would eat the good fruit and that we would cooperate with the root and become part of the tree. So in order for this to happen we have to acknowledge the root, vine and the tree with its branches, thus understand their purposeful meaning.

"Be imitators of me as I am of Christ. But above all things, my brethren, do not swear, either by heaven or by the earth, or any other oath; but let your yes be yes, your no, no; that you may not fall under judgment." (1 Cor. 11, 1 James 5:12). "You know this, my beloved brethren. But let every man be swift to hear, slow to speak, and slow to wrath. For the wrath of man does not work the justice of God. Therefore, casting aside all uncleanness and abundance of malice, with meekness receive the ingrafted word, which is able to save your souls. But be doers of the word, and not hearers only, deceiving yourselves." (James 1:19-25).

Everything I have written from the beginning to the end pertains to Jesus coming and our spiritual gifts, the garden and God's Kingdom. Jesus, the garden and the kingdom reside with and in each of us individually, spiritually and physically. All things have been growing in us individually, spiritually and physically through the Holy Spirit and the exercise of God's Almighty Power with and in Jesus Christ Crucified. Thus providing us with the pure fruit from

God, which produces in us pure spiritual life that leads us to the Total Good, thus heaven on earth, with those you love forever and ever more. "Let us rejoice: that we have been made shares in Mary's and Christ' passion. It has pleased the Father to reconcile all creation in Himself through the blood of Christ, His Son." (Divine Office Page1261). Everything that I have written about pertains to Jesus coming and our spiritual gifts from the Trinity and God's Garden and His Kingdom: That all things in us might come to full fruition with and in Jesus Christ Crucified in God's Almighty Power through the Holy Spirit. That we the living and the dead could and would come to full fruition with and in our Saviors death, His resurrection and His glorious ascension into heaven through the Holy Spirit in God's Almighty Power. Thus we the living and the dead experienced the first resurrection of the dead through the Holy Spirit with and in Jesus Christ Crucified in God's Almighty Power.

In the end we the living and the dead with and in Jesus through the Holy Spirit in God's Almighty Power by fasting and traveling at the speed of light were released from limbo and purgatory, we who were bound unjustly. We experienced spiritual death with Jesus' death in Jerusalem. We the world were set on fire by Christ's love and we were purified, we were brought to life with and in Jesus Christ through the Holy Spirit in God's Almighty Power, thus we experienced the first resurrection of the dead, we the world were set on fire and completely purified we were given a clean spirit that of Jesus' thus Jesus wrapped us with and in His love and took us with Him to heaven, we the members of Jesus' body went to limbo and purgatory with and in Him and watched Jesus raise the dead. Everyone that was with Him and in Him ascended gloriously into heaven through the Holy Spirit. And with the spirit of truth we can live with and in Jesus in the garden in His kingdom on earth forever all in God's Almighty Power.

All this is taking place within each of us individually, spiritually and physically. This scroll was written for the good of all that it would stir up faith, charity, hope and love which would produce fruit in us and enough life and enough knowledge to provoke desire for the Total Good in each of us individually; I cannot do it for you, but I can show you the "Holy Way." All restoring of faith, charity, hope and love comes from God above. I believe what is happening has all been prophesied in the Bible. That Jesus has come, will come, and will continue to come till the end of time. I don't see this as the end of our existence, only the beginning. We become the New Israel in the New Heaven and the New Earth which produces in us Heaven on Earth.

"Yes, the Lord shall comfort Zion and have pity on all her ruins; her deserts he shall make like Eden, her wasteland like the garden of the Lord; Joy and gladness shall be found in her, thanksgiving and the sound of song." (Is. 51:3).

"This desolate land has been made into a garden of Eden," they shall say. "The cities that were in ruins, laid waste, and destroyed are now repeopled and fortified." (Ez. 36:35). "Lord, free us from the dark night of death. Let the light of resurrection dawn within our hearts to bring us to the radiance of eternal life. We ask this through our Lord Jesus Christ, your Son, who lives and reigns with you and the Holy Spirit, one God, forever and ever." (Divine Office, Page 774).

"Praise to Mary, Heaven's Gate, Guiding Star of Christians' way, Mother of our Lord and king, Light and hope to souls astray.

When you heard the call of God Choosing to fulfill his plan, By your perfect act of love Hope was born in fallen man.

Help us to amend our ways, Halt the devil's strong attack, Walk with us the narrow path, Beg for us the grace we lack.

Mary, show your motherhood, Bring your children's prayers to Christ, Christ, your son, who ransomed man, Who, for us, was sacrificed.

Virgin chosen, singly blest, Ever faithful to god's call, Guide us in this earthly life, Guard us lest, deceived, we fall.

Mary, help us live our faith So that we may see your son; Join our humble prayers to yours, till life's ceaseless war is won.

Praise the father, praise the Son, Praise the holy Paraclete; Offer all through Mary's hands, Let her make our prayers complete." (Divine Office Page 1580, Song 166).

Mary the Dawn, Christ the Perfect Day; Mary the Gate, Christ the Heavenly Way!

Mary the Root, Christ the Mystic Vine; Mary the Grape, Christ the Sacred Wine!

Mary the Wheat, Christ the Living Bread, Mary the Stem, Christ the Rose blood red!

Mary the Font, Christ the Cleansing Flood; Mary the Cup, Christ the Saving Blood!

Mary the Temple, Christ the temple's Lord, Mary the Shrine, Christ the God adored!

Mary the Beacon, Christ the Haven's Rest, Mary the Mirror, Christ the Vision Blest!

Mary the Mother, Christ the mother's Son By all things blest while endless ages run.

Amen. (Divine Office Page 1579, Song 165).

Speaking from all truth, I no longer look through a dark glass I see Jesus face to face, through the Holy Spirit in God's Almighty Power. And I do see the things of heaven, because the veil was lifted. The veil was lifted by God in His Almighty Power through a vision and a dream. And Jesus was gloriously manifested with and in my husband Billy Easley through the Holy Spirit in God's Almighty Power. That God the Father revealed Himself with and in Ron Miller through the Holy Spirit. That many people in heaven are being manifested to me on earth through the Holy Spirit in God's Almighty Power.

That God in His Almighty Power with and in Jesus Christ Crucified in these last days has raised up the saints and the martyrs with His angels and has brought them with and in Him to welcome us into His Kingdom on earth through the Holy Spirit. If any one ever questions my faith, let it be said that God has raised up a very spiritual being. For me tiss the end of a futile way of life and the beginning of a new pure spiritual life with and in our Savior Jesus Christ in God's Almighty Power. For the hearer and the doer and those that do accept and believe tiss the end and the beginning also, but tiss not the end, for creation and spiritual creation continues on. Behold your fruit, eat and live. This consecration is for all unbelievers and sinners that we would be brought to conversion through the hands of Mary and given the truth with and in Jesus Christ Crucified through the Holy Spirit in God's Almighty Power.

THE LETTER OF SAINT JUDE

"Salutation* Jude, a servant of Jesus Christ and brother of James, To those who are called, who are beloved in God the Father and kept safe for Jesus Christ: May mercy, peace, and love be yours in abundance.

Occasion of the Letter* Beloved, while eagerly preparing to write to you about the salvation we share, I find it necessary to write and appeal to you to contend for the faith that was once for all entrusted to the saints. For certain intruders have stolen in among you, people who long ago were designated for this condemnation as ungodly, who pervert the grace of our God into licentiousness and deny our only Master and Lord, Jesus Christ.

Judgment on False Teachers* Now I desire to remind you, though you are fully informed, that the Lord, who once for all saved a people out of the land of

Egypt, afterward destroyed those who did not believe. And the angels who did not keep their own position, but left their proper dwelling, he has kept in eternal chains in deepest darkness for the judgment of the great Day. Likewise, Sodom and Gomorrah and the surrounding cities, which, in the same manner as they, indulged in sexual immorality and pursued unnatural lust, serve as an example buy undergoing a punishment of eternal fire.

Yet in the same way these dreamers also defile the flesh, reject authority, and slander the glorious ones. But when the archangel Michael contended with the devil and disputed about the body of Moses, he did not dare to bring a condemnation of slander against him, but said, "The Lord rebuke you!" But these people slander whatever they do not understand, and they are destroyed by those things that, like irrational animals, they know by instinct. Woe to them! For they go the way of Cain, and abandon themselves to Balaam's error for the sake of gain, and perish in Korah's rebellion.

These are blemishes on your love feasts, while they feast with you without fear, feeding themselves. They are waterless clouds carried along by the winds; autumn trees without fruit, twice dead, uprooted; wild waves of the sea, casting up the foam of their own shame; wandering stars, for whom the deepest darkness has been reserved forever.

It was also about these that Enoch, in the seventh generation from Adam, prophesied saying, "See, the Lord is coming with ten thousands of his holy ones, to execute judgment on all, and to convict everyone of all the deeds of ungodliness that they have

committed in such an ungodly way, and of all the harsh things that ungodly sinners have spoken against him. These are grumblers and malcontents; they indulge their own lusts; they are bombastic in speech, flattering people to their own advantage.

Warnings and Exhortations* But you, beloved, must remember the predictions of the apostles of our Lord Jesus Christ; for they said to you, "In the last time there will be scoffers, indulging their own ungodly lusts." It is these worldly people, devoid of the Spirit, who are causing divisions. But you, beloved, build yourselves up on your most holy faith; pray in the Holy Spirit; keep yourselves in the love of God; look forward to the mercy of our Lord Jesus Christ that leads to eternal life. And have mercy on some who are wavering; save others by snatching them out of the fire; and have mercy on still others with fear, hating even the tunic defiled by their bodies."

Benediction* Now to him who is able to keep you from falling, and to make you stand without blemish in the presence of his glory with rejoicing, to the only God our Savior, through Jesus Christ our Lord, be glory, majesty, power, and authority, before all time and now and forever, Amen." (Page 1386,1387 in the Holy Bible, nrsv.).

The Beginning of a new spiritual life and the end of Armageddon began and ended with thunder and lightning bolts, strong wind, hail, tornado warnings, and much rain. Darkness covered the earth for days. The darkness within us was conquered by light, and ended with clear skies and perfect vision. "Father in heaven, author of all truth, a people once in darkness has listened to your Word and followed your Son as he rose from the tomb. Hear the prayer of this newborn people and strengthen your Church to answer your call. May we rise and come forth into the light of day to stand in your presence until eternity dawns. We ask this through Christ our Lord." (Divine Office pages 477,478).

Cathryn Lucille Easley

I am very proud and honored to share with all God's children the gifts and insight he has given me. I hope everyone that sees these pictures enjoys them as much as I do, that in some way God and the living body of Christ might have made a difference in someone's life. Peace, it is I. Do not be afraid.

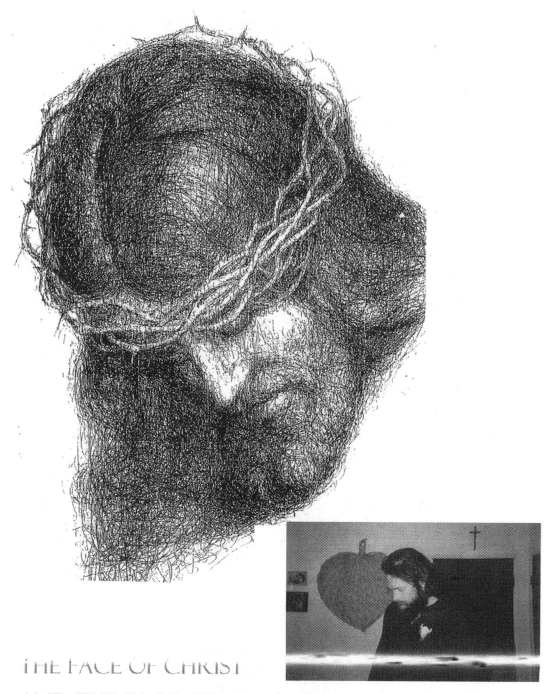

THE FACE OF CHRIST
AND THE FACE OF MY HUSBAND BILLY EASLEY

The Angels that I see and have in my life. (From left to right)
Jack Kroninger, Robert Lyons, Tyler Robillard, Jade Burkhart-
Wesolowki, Kylee Kragrud, Larrissa Jenkins, Katelyn Kragurd,
Kayla Lindqist, Billie Jo Easley, DeLanee Jamie, Krista
Burkhart-Wesolowki and my dog Missy.

DeEdra Manning, Cip Spoon

HANNAH CUPP

THE PEOPLE I SEE TODAY THAT
LIVE IN HEAVEN ON EARTH.

SAINT AARON

AARON POLIFKA

ABIGAIL FROM
THE OLD TESTAMENT

AMANDA ABIGAIL DALEY

FATHER ABRAHAM

LES

ST. ALBERT THE GREAT

BILLY'S DAD ALBERT EASLEY

SAINT ALFRED THE GREAT

FATHER AL DAWE

ST. ALAN

ALAN AND BRENDA STONE
MY HUSBANDS COUSINS

ST. AMATA

MY NIECE AMY MCINTEER

ST. ANN

MY MOM ANN BISHOP

ST. ANNA THE PROPHETESS

ANNA MARIE DRESDEN

ST. ANNE

STEPHANIE WRIGHT

ST. ANTHONY OF PADUA

ANTHONY JENKINS

ST. ANSELM

TOM MELLINGER

ST. AUGUSTINE

AUGIE MARTONE

APOSTLE ANDREW

ANDREW MURPHY

APOSTLE BARTHOLOMEW

NATE BURRIS

APOSTLE JAMES THE GREATER

CHRISTINE MY DAUGHTER IN LAW
JOLEANE AND BILLIE JO MY DAUGHTERS
AND MY SON JAMES WALKER

APOSTLE
JAMES THE LESS

MY BROTHER
GENE MCINTEER

APOSTLE JOHN

MY SON JASON WALKER
AND MY MOM ANN

APOSTLE JUDE

MY SON OMAR EASLEY

APOSTLE MATTHEW

MATTHEW CLASSEN

APOSTLE MATTHIAS

MATTHEW LAIDLER

APOSTLE PETER

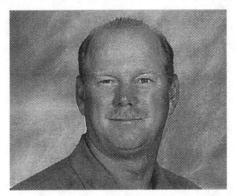

PETER TREVILLIAN

APOSTLE PHILLIP

PHILLIP WINTER

APOSTLE THOMAS

MY SON QUENTIN EASLEY

APOSTLE SIMON
THE ZEALOT

MY NEPHEW
SCOTT BURRILL

ST. BARBARA

BARBARA KNOWLES

BLESSED BARTOLO LONGO

JAMES ROY SMITH

ST. BEDE

CODY BALDWIN

ST. ROBERT BELLERMINE

MY BROTHER IN LAW
ROBERT BURRILL

ST. BENEDICT

BLAIR HILLIG

ST. BENJAMIN

BENJAMIN HUNICKE
HE ALSO REMINDS ME OF BENJAMIN FRANKLIN

ST. BERNADETTE

BILL'S SISTER
ANNETTE EASLEY GESINO

BLESSED BRIAN

BRIAN YAEGER

St. Bridget of Sweden

My Daughter Billie Jo II Easley

"For a long time St. Bridget wanted to know the number of blows Our Lord received during His Passion. He one day appeared to her and said: "I received 5480 blows on My Body. If you wish to honor them in some way, say 15 Our Fathers and 15 Hail Marys with the following prayers (which He taught her) for a whole year. When the year is up,, you will have honored each one of My wounds."

PROMISES

l. I will deliver 15 souls of his lineage from purgatory. 2. 15 souls of his lineage will be confirmed and preserved in grace. 3. 15 sinners of his lineage will be converted. 4. Whoever recites these prayers will attain the first degree of perfection. 5. 15 days before his death I will give him My Precious Body in order that he may escape eternal starvation; I will give him My Precious Blood to drink lest he thirst eternally. 6. 15 days before his death he will feel a deep contrition for all his sins and will have a perfect knowledge of them. 7. I will place before him the sign of My Victorious Cross for his help and defense against the attacks of his enemies. 8. Before his death I shall come with My dearest beloved Mother. 9. I shall graciously receive his soul, and will lead it into eternal joys. 10. And having led it there I shall give him a special draught from the fountain of My Deity, something I will not for those who have not recited My prayers. 11. Let it be known that whoever may have been living in a state of mortal sin for 30 years, but who will recite devoutly, or have the intention to recite these Prayers, the Lord will forgive him all his sins. 12. I shall protect him from strong temptations. 13. I shall preserve and guard his 5 senses. 14. I shall preserve him from a sudden death. 15. His soul will be delivered from eternal death. 16. He will obtain all he asks for from God and the Blessed Virgin. 17. If he has lived all his life doing his own will and he is to die the next day, his life will be prolonged. 18. Every time one recites these Prayers he gains 199 days indulgence. 19. He is assured of being joined to the supreme Choir of Angels. 20. Whoever teaches these Payers to another, will have continuous joy and merit which will endure eternally. 21. There where these Prayers are being said or will be said in the future, God is present with His grace. The Church has always recommended meditations on the Passion of Our Lord. The Blessed Virgin Mary said to St. Bridget: "The consideration of the Passion of my Son ought to be frequently in man's thoughts." St. Bonaventure said: "Let him who desires to attain union with God keep the eyes of his soul ever fixed on Him who hangs dying on the Cross. It's from those wounds of the Saviour that man draws power to suffer not merely with patience but with joy."

FIFTEEN ST. BRIGET PRAYERS

First Prayer

Our Father – Hail Mary, O Jesus Christ! Eternal Sweetness to those who love Thee, joy surpassing all joy and all desire, salvation and hope of all sinners, Who hast proved that Thou hast no greater desire than to be among men, even assuming human nature at the fullness of time for the love of men! Recall all the sufferings Thou hast endured from the instant of Thy conception, and especially during Thy Passion, as it was decreed and ordained from all eternity in the Divine plan. Remember, O Lord, that during the last Supper with Thy disciples, having washed their feet, Thou gavest them Thy Most Precious Body and Blood, and while at the same time Thou didst sweetly console them, Thou didst foretell them Thy coming Passion. Remember the sadness and bitterness which Thou didst experience in Thy Soul as Thou Thyself bore witness saying: "My Soul is sorrowful, even unto death." Remember all the fear, anguish and pain that Thou didst suffer in Thy delicate Body before the torment of the Crucifixion when, after having prayed three times, bathed in a sweat of blood, Thou wast betrayed by Judas, Thy disciple, arrested by the people of a nation Thou hadst chosen and elevated, accused by false witnesses, unjustly judged by three judges during the flower of Thy youth and during the solemn Paschal season. Remember that Thou wast despoiled of Thy garments and clothed in those of derision; that Thy Face and Eyes were veiled; that Thou wast buffeted, crowned with thorns, a reed placed in Thy Hands; that Thou was crushed with blows and overwhelmed with affronts and outrages. In memory of all these pains and sufferings which Thou didst endure before Thy Passion on the Cross, grant me before my death true contrition, a sincere and entire confession, worthy satisfaction and the remission of all my sins. Amen.

Second Prayer, Our Father -- Hail Mary. O Jesus! True liberty of angels, Paradise of delights! Remember the horror and sadness which Thou didst endure when Thy enemies, like furious lions, surrounded Thee, and by thousands of insults, spits, blows, lacerations and other unheard-of-cruelties, tormented Thee at will. In consideration of these torments and insulting words, I beseech Thee, O my Savior, to deliver me from all my enemies, visible and invisible, and to bring me, under Thy protection, to the perfection of eternal salvation. Amen.

Third Prayer, Our Father – Hail Mary. O Jesus! Creator of heaven and earth Whom nothing can encompass or limit, Thou Who dost enfold and hold all under Thy loving power! Remember the very bitter pain Thou didst suffer when the Jews nailed Thy Sacred Hands and Feet to the Cross by blow after blow with big blunt nails, and not finding Thee in a pitiable enough state to satisfy their rage, they enlarged Thy Wounds, and added pain to pain, and with indescribable cruelty stretched Thy Body on the Cross, pulled Thee from all sides, thus dislocating Thy Limbs. I beg of Thee, O Jesus, by the memory of this most loving suffering of the Cross, to grant me the grace to fear Thee and to love Thee. Amen.

Fourth Prayer, Our Father – Hail Mary. O Jesus! Heavenly Physician, raised aloft on the Cross to heal our wounds with Thine! Remember the bruises which Thou didst suffer and the weakness of all Thy Members which were distended to such a degree that never was there pain like unto Thine. From the crown of Thy Head to the soles of Thy Feet there was not one spot on Thy Body that was not in torment; and yet, forgetting all Thy sufferings, Thou didst not cease to pray to Thy heavenly Father for Thy enemies, saying: "Father forgive them, for they know not what they do." Through this great mercy, and in memory of this suffering, grant that the remembrance of Thy most bitter Passion may effect in me a perfect contrition and the remission of all my sins. Amen.

Fifth Prayer, Our Father – Hail Mary. O Jesus! Mirror of eternal splendor! Remember the sadness which Thou experienced when, contemplating in the light of Thy Divinity the predestination of those who would be saved by the merits of Thy Sacred Passion, Thou didst see at the same time, the great multitude of reprobates who would be damned for their sins, and Thou didst complain bitterly of those hopeless, lost and unfortunate sinners. Through this abyss of compassion and pity, and especially through the goodness which Thou displayed to the good thief when Thou saidst to him: "This day, thou shalt be with Me in paradise." I beg of Thee, O Sweet Jesus, that at the hour of my death, Thou wilt show me mercy. Amen.

Sixth Prayer, Our Father – Hail Mary. O Jesus! Beloved and most desirable King! Remember the grief Thou didst suffer when, naked and like a common criminal, Thou was fastened and raised on the Cross, when all Thy relatives and friends abandoned Thee, except Thy beloved Mother, who remained close to Thee during Thy agony and whom Thou didst entrust to Thy faithful disciple when Thou saidst to Mary: "Woman, behold thy son!: and to St. John: "Son, behold thy Mother!" I beg of Thee, O my Saviour, by the sword of sorrow which pierced the soul of Thy holy Mother, to have compassion on me in all my afflictions and tribulations, both corporal and spiritual, and to assist me in all my trials, and especially at the hour of my death. Amen.

Seventh Prayer, Our Father – Hail Mary. O Jesus! Inexhaustible Fountain of compassion, Who by a profound gesture of love said from the Cross: "I thirst!" suffered from the thirst for the salvation of the human race. I beg of Thee, O my Saviour, to inflame in my heart the desire to tend toward perfection in all my acts, and to extinguish in me the concupiscence of the flesh and the ardor of worldly desires. Amen.

Eighth Prayer, Our Father – Hail Mary. O Jesus! Sweetness of hearts, delight of the spirit! By the bitterness of the vinegar and gall which Thou didst taste on the Cross for love of us, grant me the grace to receive worthily Thy Precious Body and Blood during my life and at the hour of my death, that they may serve as a remedy and consolation for my soul. Amen.

Ninth Prayer, Our Father – Hail Mary. O Jesus! Royal virtue, joy of the mind! Recall the pain Thou didst endure when, plunged in an ocean of bitterness at the approach of death, insulted, outraged by the Jews, Thou didst cry out in a loud voice that Thou was abandoned by Thy Father, saying: "My God, My God, why hast Thou forsaken me?"

Tenth Prayer, Our Father – Hail Mary. O Jesus! Who art the beginning and end of all things, life and virtue! Remember that for my sake Thou was plunged in an abyss of suffering from the soles of Thy feet to the crown of The Head. In consideration of the enormity of Thy Wounds, teach me to keep, through pure love, Thy Commandments, whose way is wide and easy for those who love Thee. Amen.

Eleventh Prayer, Our Father – Hail Mary. O Jesus! Deep abyss of mercy! I beg of Thee, in memory of Thy Wounds which penetrated to the very marrow of Thy Bones and to the depth of Thy being, to draw me, a miserable sinner overwhelmed by my offenses, away from sin and to hide me from Thy Face justly irritated against me. Hide me in Thy Wounds until Thy anger and just indignation shall have passed away. Amen.

Twelfth Prayer, Our Father – Hail Mary. O Jesus! Mirror of truth, symbol of unity, link of charity! Remember the multitude of wounds with which Thou was covered from Head to Foot, torn and reddened by the spilling of Thy adorable Blood. O Great and Universal Pain which Thou didst suffer in Thy virginal Flesh for love of us! Sweetest Jesus! What is there that Thou couldst have done for us which Thou has not done? May the fruit of Thy Sufferings be renewed in my soul by the faithful remembrance of Thy Passion, and may Thy Love increase in my heart each day, until I see Thee in eternity, Thou Who art the treasury of every real good and every joy, which I beg Thee to, grant me, O Sweetest Jesus, in heaven. Amen.

Thirteenth Prayer, Our Father – Hail May. O Jesus! Strong Lion, Immortal and invincible King! Remember the pain which Thou didst endure! When all Thy strength, both moral and physical, was entirely exhausted, Thou didst bow Thy Head, saying: "It is consummated!" Through this anguish and grief, I beg of Thee, Lord Jesus, to have mercy on me at the hour of my death when my mind will be greatly troubled and my soul will be in anguish. Amen.

Fourteenth Prayer, Our Father – Hail Mary. O Jesus! Only Son of the Father, Splendor and Figure of His Substance! Remember the simple and humble recommendation Thou didst make of Thy Soul to They Eternal Father, saying: "Father, into Thy Hands I commend My Spirit!" And with Thy Body all torn, and Thy Heart broken, and the bowels of Thy Mercy open to redeem us, Thou didst expire. By this Precious Death, I beg of Thee, O King of Saints, to comfort me and help me to resist the devil, the flesh and the world, so that being dead to the world I may live for Thee alone, I beg of Thee, at the hour of my death to receive me, a pilgrim and an exile returning to Thee, Amen.

Fifteenth Prayer, Our Father – Hail Mary. O Jesus! True and fruitful Vine! Remember the abundant outpouring of Blood which Thou didst so generously shed from

Thy Sacred Body, as juice from grapes in a wine press. From Thy Side, pierced with a lance by a soldier, blood and water issued forth until there was not left in Thy Body a single drop; and finally, like a bundle of myrrh lifted to the top of the Cross, Thy delicate Flesh was destroyed, the very Substance of Thy Body withered, and the Marrow of Thy Bones dried up. Through this bitter Passion and through the outpouring of Thy Precious Blood, I beg of Thee, O Sweet Jesus, to receive my soul when I am in my death agony. Amen. Conclusion, O Sweet Jesus! Pierce my heart so that my tears of penitence and love will be my bread day and night. May I be converted entirely to Thee; may my heart be Thy perpetual habitation; may my conversation be pleasing to Thee; and may the end of my life be so praiseworthy that I may merit heaven and there with Thy saints, praise Thee forever. Amen.

(Pieta Prayer Book)

ST. BOSCO

ROSCO LUGGIEVI AND MY HUSBAND BILLY
MY DAUGHTER DAISY AND BILLIE JO

ST. BRUNO

MARK BRUNO
HIS SISTER HEIDI
AND HIS DAUGHTER CODY

ST. BRUNO

LARRY BRUNO
HIS DAUGHTER KARRY
AND ROYSE AND CODY

ST. BRUNO SEGNI

JEFF AND KARRY BRUNO

ST BURIANA

BRIANA WILLIAMS

CANDICE
THE ETHIOPIAN QUEEN

MY NIECE
CANDICE BURRILL LUNDY

ST. CAMILLA

CAMRIE HUNICKE

ST. CATHERINE
LABOURE

CATHY EASLEY
AND MY HUSBAND BILLY

ST. CATHERINE OF SIENA

CATHERINE DIMITRY

ST. CECIL

CECIL WALL

ST. CHARLES

BILLY'S BROTHER
CHARLES EASLEY

ST. CHRISTINA

MY NIECE
CHRISTINA MCINTEER YAEGER

ST. CHRISTOPHER

MY NEPHEW
CHRISTOPHER GESINO

ST. JOHN CHRYSOSTOM

MIKE BIRD

ST. CLARE

CLARE TESTA WALL

ST. COLETTE

COLEEN BURKHART

SAINT COSMAS

SAMUEL CASTILLO

ST. JOHN OF DAMASCUS

JAKE WISEHAR

PROPHET DANIEL

MY NEPHEW DANIEL EASLEY
AND HIS GRANDMA AND MOM

DEBORAH THE PROPHETESS

MY SISTER DEBBIE EVANS

ST. DENIS

DENNIS JENKINS

BLESSED DIANE

DIANE WAYMAN EASLEY

ST. DONATA

DONNA O'BRIEN

ST. DOROTHY

DOROTHY MANCHA

ST. EDWARD

EDWARD HOUSWORTH

ST. ELIZABETH OF PORTUGAL

DIANE WILSON

ST. ELIZABETH OF HUNGARY

JACKIE WILSON

EMORUN
ST. ANNES GRANDMOTHER

SIMONITA GONZALES

ESTHER

MY NEPHEW'S WIFE
SUSAN ESTHERMCINTEER
MICHAEL, MICHAEL JR AND ALEXIS

ST. EVA

MY STEPMOM
EVELYN SHEAMAN WALL

PROPHET EZEKIEL

MY NEPHEW EZEKIEL EASLEY

ST. MARIA FAUSTINA KOWALSKA

KAREN CHOLEY

MOTHER MICHAELA MOORACZEWSKA

NURSE CHRIS SKORICK

ST. FELICITY

SHAYNA WRIGHT

ST. FRANCES OF ROME

FRANCES KLINE

ST. FRANCIS OF ASSISI

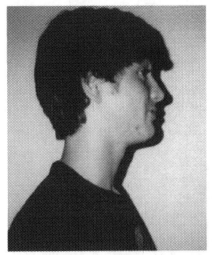

MY SON OMAR FRANCIS EASLEY

BLESSED FRANCISCO MARTO

WILLIAM WAIT

ST. GENEVIEVE

GENEVIEVE JENKINS

ST. GERARD MANJELLA

CORY DRAPER

ST. GERTRUDE

GERTRUDE

152

ST. GEORGE

GEORGE MARTINEZ

BLESSED GIACOMO CUSMANO

ROBERT

SAINT GUY

GUY EASLEY AND HIS SISTER,
CASSIE CALHOUN

ST. GWEN

GWENDOLINE CASTILLO

ISMERIA ST. ANNES MOM

DULCINA MARIE GONZALES

ST. HELEN

HELEN DICKERSON

ST. HALLVARD

MY STEPDAD CLAY HALL

PROPHET ISAAC

MY NEPHEW ISAAC EASLEY

JUDY GARLAND

DELANEE JAMIE

PROPHET JEREMIAH

ALLIE, KIMBERLY
AND JEREMY WARTENBERG

PROPHET JOSHUA

MY NEPHEW JOSHUA EASLEY

PROPHETESS JUDITH

JUDY CARTWRIGHT

ST. JEROME

MY DAD CLIFTON WALL

ST. JEROME EMILIANI

AMOLIO MURILLO

ST. JOAN OF ARC

MY DAUGHTER DAISY ROSE EASLEY

ST. JOAN DE LESTONNAC

MY SISTER
JOANIE EVANS MCDANIELS

ST. JOHN LEONARDI

JOHN MIKE MCINTEER

BLESSED JOHN NELSON

JOHN NELSON

ST. JOHN NEUMANN

FATHER LARRY BAUMANN

ST. JULIE BILLIART

ROSEY DRISCOLL

ST. JULIAN

JULIAN FRANCIS

ST. JUSTIN

JUSTIN HAMMONS

St. Kevin

Kevin Cartwright

St. Lazarus

A. Joseph Zambito

ST. LAURA

BILLY EASLEY AND HIS MOM
LAURA BEASANT SLOUGH

BLESSED LAURA

LAURA DUNCAN

ST. LAURENTIA

LE LE AND LAUREEN PELAEZ

ST. LAWRENCE

LARRY AND SHEILA LAIDLER

ST. LEO THE GREAT

LEO NEMTSOVICH, MOM, WIFE AND DAUGHTER

ST. LUCY

CATHRYN EASLEY
AND MY GRANDSON
JONAH WALKER

ST. LUKE

DAKOTA TEAGHON

ST. MARIE MARGUERITE
D'YOUBILLE

DONNA SPINA

BLESSED MARIE-ROSE DUROCHER

MS. KNOWS THE GROUND

ST. MAROELLINUS

BOYD DURHAM

ST. MARGERATE OF CORTONA

MARTHA   MEIGHAN

MARIA PORTINARI
AND DAUGHTER

MARIA AND ANN CUNDISS

ST. MARIA GORETTI

BREANN HERNANDEZ

ST. MARK

JOHN

STS. MARY MAGDALENE AND MARTHA

ROSE PIZZANO & JEANNE KOCHAN

ST. MARTIAL

MARTIAL

ST. MARTIN I

NICK VANDERHADEN

ST. MARY CLEOPHAS

MY SISTER MARY LOU BURRILL

ST. MATILDA

MATILDA NUIEZ

ST. MICHAEL

MY NEPHEW MICHAEL MCINTEER
HE ALSO REMINDS ME OF
MARQUIS LAURENT DE GOUVION - ST. CYR

ST. MEINARD

MAYNARD FONDA

ST. PAUL MIKI

ROBERT MACKAWA

ST. MELANIA

AL & MALENA PERAZA
MALIA AND JOEL

NATALIE DE LABORDE DE MEREVILLE,
COMTESSE CHARLES DE NOAILLES

MY NIECE JENNIFER VODIKA
AND CASTON AND ROCCO

ST. NEREUS, ST. ACHILLEUS

ABELINO, VICTORIA, MARIA
AND ABELINO III CARBAJAL

ST. NICHOLAS

NICHOLAS
WOLFGANG DOLHYJ

ST. NICHOLAS OF TOLENTINE

MY NEPHEW
NICHOLAS MCINTEER
AND MY DAUGHTER DAISY

ST. NINO

MY SISTER IN LAW
CHRISITINA FRIEDEL WALL

ST. OLIVIA

OLIVIA LAIPPLE

ST. PANCRAS

BRANDON

SAINT PAUL

PAUL WRIGHT

ST. PAUL CHONG HASANG

ROBERT LYONS

ST. PAULINA

PAULETTE MARTONE

ST. PHILIP NERI

PHILIP WINTER

ST. PRISCILLA

PRISCILLA BURKHART

ST. PUDENS

BOB BURKHART

ST. RITA OF CASCIA

SERITA GUTIAERREZ

ST. RONALD

R ON BISHOP
AND MY MOM ANN

PROPHET SAMUEL

SAM KOHLER

ST. SARAH

MY NIECE SARAH EASLEY

ST. SCHOLASTICA

KAREN MCGRANE

ST. ELIZABETH
ANN SETON

JENNIFER WRIGHT

THE PROPHET SIMEON
THE HOLY MAN

DON ROWLEY

ST. STEPHEN

STEPHEN OTERRO

ST. TERESA OF AVILA

TERESE KRUCEK

ST. TERESA ~
THE LITTLE FLOWER

KATIE WRIGHT

JOANNE BECKER

ST. THEODORE

THEODORE
WILLIAM GESINO

ST. TIMOTHY

TIM WERNER

ST. THOMAS AQUINAS

MY SON
QUENTIN THOR EASLEY

ST. TUTILO

TUTILO VIANELLO

ST. VICTORIA

MY SISTER IN LAW
VICKY VODIKA MCINTEER

Anna's second husband is taller and older then Joachim was. His name is Eliud, and he had a post at the temple connected with the supervision of the sacrificial animals. Anna had a daughter by him, also called Mary. At Christ's birth she must have been 6 or 8 years old. Eliud died soon after this, and it was God's will that Anna should marry for a third time. Of this marriage that was a son, who was called one of Christ's breathern.

Information taken from the book called: The Life of the Blessed Virgin Mary – From the Visions of Ven. Ann Catherine Emmerich. Page 277 and the Genealogical Table from the last page of this book.

MY BROTHER CLIFTON WALL

These are some of my family members
(left to right)
Jason Walker, Mary and Bob Burrill, Billy Easley, Amanda Daley,
Ann Bishop, Joleane Easley, Quentin Easley, James and Christine
Walker, Jesse Butterfield, Billie Jo Easley, missing Omar and
Daisy Easley

For up to date messages from Heaven
go to www.Holylove.org

REFERENCES

Mysteries of the Glory Unveiled, Copyright 2000 by David Herzog. Published by McDougal Publishing. ISBN 1-58158-012-6. My email is cathy.easley@yahoo.com. And I attend church at St. Germaine in Prescott Valley, Arizona.

Little Office of the Blessed Virgin Mary, Copyright 1988 by Catholic Book Publishing Corp., ISBN 978-0-89942-450-7.

Divine Office, Copyright 1985, 1976 by Catholic Book Publishing Corp. (T-407).

Modern Catholic Dictionary by John A. Hardon, Copyright 1980. Published by Doubleday. ISBN 0-385-12162-8

The Catholic Teen Bible, Copyright 2004 by Our Sunday Visitor Publishing Division.

Holy Bible, The New Revised Standard Version Bible, Copyright 1989 by American Bible Society.

Spurgeon's Morning by Morning, Copyright 2007 by Alistair Begg. Published by Crossway Books. ISBN 978-1-4335-1358-9.

Spurgeon's Evening by Evening, Copyright 2007 by Alistair Begg. Published by Crossway Books. ISBN 978-1-4335-1359-6.

Catechism Of The Catholic Church, Copyright 1994. Published by Doubleday. ISBN 0-385-50819-0.

Go to allposter.com in reference to number 6805075.

Holy Bible King James Version, Copyright 1979. Published by The Church Of Jesus Christ Of Latter-Day Saints Salt Lake City, Utah.

Summa Theologiae by Thomas Aquinas, Copyright 1989 by Timothy McDermott. Published by Christian Classics. ISBN 0-87061-210-7.

His Holiness John Paul II Crossing The Threshold Of Hope, Copyright 1994 by Arnoldo Nomdadori Editore. Published by Random House. ISBN 0-679-44084-4.

The Father Speaks To His Children Copyright 1999 by Mother Eugenia. Published by Pater Publications – C.P. 135 – 67100 L'Aquila (Italy).

Holy Bible New American Edition, Copyright 1970. Published by the Confraternity of Christian Doctrine, with Concordance and Dictionary.

The Life Of The Blessed Virgin Mary, Copyright 1954. Published by Burns and Oates. ISBN 978-0-89555-048-4.

My Daily Reading from the New Testament and Daily Mass Book, Copyright 1941 by Father Stedman. Published by Confraternity of the Precious Blood.

The Pieta Prayer Book, Copyright 2006 Published by Miraculous Lady Of Roses, LLC.

The picture of Our Lady of Sorrow by Quentin Easley 2011.

The picture of the Exaltation of Jesus Christ by Omar Easley 2008.